REAL ESTATE
TECHNOLOGY
GUIDE

Saul D. Klein
John W. Reilly
Mike Barnett

Dearborn™
Real Estate Education

President: Roy Lipner
Publisher: Evan Butterfield
Managing Editor, Print Products: Louise Benzer
Development Editor: Christopher Oler
Production Coordinator: Daniel Frey
Quality Assurance Editor: David Shaw
Typesetter: Ellen Gurak
Creative Director: Lucy Jenkins

Published by Dearborn™ Real Estate Education, a division of Dearborn Financial Publishing, Inc.®
30 South Wacker Drive
Chicago, IL 60606-7481
(312) 836-4400
http://www.dearbornRE.com

Printed in the United States of America.

04 05 06 10 9 8 7 6 5 4 3 2 1

Library of Congress Cataloging-in-Publication Data

Klein, Saul D.
    Real estate technology guide / Saul D. Klein, John W. Reilly, Mike Barnett.
        p. cm.
    ISBN 0-7931-7732-4
        1. Real estate business—Computer network resources.   2. Internet.
3. Web sites.   I. Reilly, John W.   II. Barnett, Michael, 1947-   III. Title.
    HD1380.6.K58 2004
    333.33'0285'4678–dc22   2003025775

Contents ■

Dedicated to . . . Janie, Patty, and Phyllis . . . and to our families . . . who allow us the time to pursue our passion and our "crusade," doing all we can to make the world smaller by "connecting" as many people as possible.

Winning in real estate is about attitude. Commitment is key. Successful real estate professionals are those who have a positive outlook on life and business and are self-motivated and seriously committed to success. Are you moderately committed or seriously committed to success? The difference will be seen in the result. A case in point: Whom would you want performing CPR on you should you ever need it—someone who is moderately committed or seriously committed?

Commitment requires decision making. When you decide you want to do something, often the decision itself moves you closer to the goal. As W.H. Murray notes in *The Scottish Himalayan Expedition:*

> *Until one is committed there is hesitance, the chance to draw back, always ineffectiveness. Concerning all acts of initiative (and creation) there is one elementary truth, the ignorance of which kills countless ideas and splendid plans: That the moment one definitely commits oneself, then providence moves too. All sorts of things occur to help one that would otherwise never have occurred. A whole stream of events issues from the decision, raising in one's favor all manner of unforeseen incidents and meetings and material assistance, which no man could have dreamt would have come his way. I have learned a deep respect for Goethe's couplets:*
>
> *"Whatever you can do, or dream you can. Begin it ... boldness has genius, power and magic in it."*

Winning in real estate is about consistency. Success requires consistent marketing of services to potential buyers and sellers while delivering services to current customers and clients. In many instances, your marketing efforts today will not produce immediate results. Nevertheless, your marketing effort should be directed toward creating "clients for life" and a steady stream of referral business from your clients and real estate associates.

As technology continues to provide real estate professionals with new tools with new capabilities and potential, the limiting factor becomes the ability to learn how to use new technology and put it to work in business, often with no immediate or visible "return on investment."

Success in utilizing technology requires motivation, perseverance, and serious commitment. Each chapter of this book thus begins with a motivational quote from Dr. Denis Waitley, one of the top motivational authors and speakers in the country. More motivational resources can be found at *http://Motivation.RealTown.com*.

The *Real Estate Technology Guide* is a revolutionary approach to conventional publishing. It combines printed material with the World Wide Web and online communities. It provides links to expanded materials that serve as resources and keep much of the content current and relevant. This is accomplished not simply by using links to Web content controlled by others, but by maintaining control of these links by using third-level domains, a concept discussed in detail and applicable to the administration of a successful Internet strategy. The *Real Estate Technology Guide* is more than a book—it is an interactive, three-dimensional learning experience.

The book portion of this approach presents the Internet and technology in 18 chapters. The text includes a glossary that not only has important professional technology terms, but popularly-used words and phrases. It also features tips, checklists, and the above mentioned links to more in-depth information.

To reap the most benefit from this approach, it is useful to keep in mind the following underlying themes:

1. Using technology will make you more efficient, effective, *and visible*. One of the keys to success in real estate sales and marketing is standing out from the competition. As many in the real estate business are "technology averse," the use of technology in your business will appeal to the needs of the technology savvy consumer, and differentiate you from your competition.
2. It's easy when you know how. Technology comprises a large, broad body of information. Most of the technology used by real estate practitioners on a daily basis is not complex; nevertheless, there is a learning curve with all technology hardware and software. New technologies may seem very difficult until you learn how they work and how you will use them in your business. Mastering most technology skills you will use in your business requires nothing more than a little instruction and a little practice. After that, it's easy.

3. It's the little things that make a difference. Facility with technology is not an all-or-nothing proposition. You do not need to learn everything about technology before you can begin to benefit from its use in your real estate business. As you learn little tips and tricks, put them to use right away—in the long run, it will make a big difference in your business.

4. Integrate technology into what you are already doing. Many of the things you are doing right now in your business can be automated. As you are tempted to purchase new technology for your business, make sure it can be integrated into your current business practices.

5. Many technology products and services you now pay for but are not using. Use the technology you are already paying for before expanding. Many real estate professionals underutilize many technological products and services they own or are renting on a continuing basis; many have not mastered even half of the potential of the MLS technology provided (for a fee) by their MLS vendors. When is the last time you made a complete list of the functionality provided by your MLS vendor and inventoried your skills against it?

A number of trademarked brands appear in this text. To ensure a smooth reading experience, we list the companies and software here and do not include the ® or ™ symbols to indicate their reserved rights. All rights that accompany both designations are recognized in this introduction. The use of these company names does not imply active involvement or endorsement of this text.

Acrobat	Flash	QuickTime
ACT!	FrontPage	Shockwave
Adobe	Goldmine	SPAM (the Hormel
Advantage Express	Hewlett-Packard	food product)
Agent2000	Homesite	Supra iBox
AgentOffice	Kodak	Tide
Amazon.com	Listserv	Top Producer
AOL	McAfee	Wite-Out
Apple	Norton	Windows
AT&T	PageMaker	WINForms
Blackberry	Palm Pilot	WinZip
Coca-Cola	PKZip	Word
Consumer Guide	PowerPoint	World Merge
DreamWeaver	PREP	Yahoo
Eudora	Quickbooks	ZipForm
Excel	Quicken	
FedEx		

So with that, you are ready to begin . . . have fun and we'll see you on the Internet.

Saul, John, and Mike

■ About the Authors

Saul D. Klein, President of InternetCrusade, is an internationally recognized speaker who has spent more than 15,000 hours in front of real estate professionals and consumers. He is a past President of the San Diego Association of REALTORS® and served as a Director to the California Association of REALTORS® from 1991 to 1997. Saul is the author of several real estate courses, including courses in ethics, agency, and financial and tax planning for the real estate professional. In the last 14 years, Saul has traveled over 1 million miles delivering a message on technology and its role in the future of the real estate industry. In 2003, Saul was named one of the "25 Most Influential People in Real Estate" by REALTOR® Magazine. The magazine credited Internet-Crusade for the successful turnaround of the National Association of REALTOR®'s e-Pro designation and the building of some of the most popular online communities in real estate.

John W. Reilly, InternetCrusade Vice President of Publishing, is a member of both the California and Hawaii State Bar Associations. His involvement in real estate education stretches back 30 years. In addition to conducting seminars to licensees, escrow officers and attorneys, John was an adjunct professor of Real Estate Law at the University of Hawaii Richardson School of Law for ten years. The Real Estate Educators Association (REEA) named him National Educator of the Year in 1990. John served as President of REEA in 1988. His book *The Language of Real Estate* is a national best-seller and now in its fifth edition. In addition, John is the author of *Fundamentals for a Strong Foundation* and *Contracts & You*, published by REEPco, as well as *Agency Relationships in Real Estate, Consensual Dual Agency,* and *Questions and Answers to Help You Pass the Real Estate Exam,* all published by Dearborn Publishing.

Mike Barnett is one of the most sought after talents in the technology world. Though he is known internationally for his abilities in technology, Mike is also the fourth generation of his family to work in real estate. He has distinguished himself in real estate education, receiving Honorable Mention for NAR Educator of the Year in 1997. Mike was President of the Arizona Chapter of the Real Estate Educators Association and Director of the Scottsdale and Arizona Association of Realtors. As Vice President of Technology for the InternetCrusade, he oversees the day-to-day technology operation of the company and also leads the development of all new technologies and solutions. Mike specializes in Domain Name Space (DNS system) connectivity and e-mail.

Chapter One

Technology, the Internet, and the Real Estate Business

Real success comes in small portions day by day.
DENIS WAITLEY
http://Motivation.InternetCrusade.com

■ INTRODUCTION

The marketing, sale, and transfer of real estate revolve around the exchange of information about property and people. Today's technology allows data to be transferred in a faster, more cost-effective way than in the past. Successful real estate practitioners will continue to be those who use technology and the **Internet** to gather, sort, add value, and distribute all information pertaining to the people and property in a real estate transaction.

Also key, at every step in the process, is communication between all parties to the transaction. From licensee to seller, buyer to licensee, buyer to seller, and buyer and seller to lender and other transaction participants, effective communications can make the difference between success and failure. Internet technologies add a new dimension to communication.

In many ways, technology is changing the way consumers search for real estate and the way they communicate with their **real estate professional** and other participants in the home purchase process. The National Association of REALTORS® 2003 Survey of Home Buyers and Sellers reveals that 71 percent of homebuyers use the Internet in their search for a home, up from 62 percent in 2002.

1

Continuing success in real estate often depends on one's ability to differentiate oneself from the competition. Real estate is a "me too" business. From the public's perspective, most of the things a real estate professional does to sell a piece of property are the same things all real estate professionals do—MLS, lockbox, For Sale sign, open house, classified ads. If what you do to sell a property is the same as everyone else does, other than commission structure, why should a seller or buyer work with you instead of your competition?

LITTLE THINGS MAKE A DIFFERENCE

Like real estate in general, when it comes to the use of technology, "the little things make a difference." Technology is not an all or nothing proposition. As you learn new technologies or technology-related skills, it is important to put them to work immediately and they will, in time, have an impact on your business and your success. This book is full of little things, which, if implemented, will affect your bottom line and your longevity in real estate. Remember, it is not doing everything, but doing little things, that will make your service to consumers different from those of your competition.

As you are well aware, the real estate business is one of many little things. Each transaction is a myriad of little things that lead to the biggest thing in most people's lives, the purchase of a home.

The integration of technology into your business will help you create a compelling argument or a value proposition for hiring you instead of your competition. While many real estate professionals resist adopting technology, those who do so immediately set themselves apart from their competition.

Most real estate professionals across the country are experiencing downward pressure on commissions. While pricing is a legitimate way to compete, there are other methods. Bringing your clients and customers convenience and quality service will go a long way toward helping you substantiate your fees. Using technology with a technology-inclined customer, the **connected consumer,** will add value to your services and help you establish your compelling argument.

Integrating technology into one's business often seems like a mountain too big to climb. It is not. Just remember, it is easy when you know how. While it is not the intent of this book to teach you everything about technology, it is the intent to teach you how to integrate technology into your existing business to maximize the effectiveness of technology as you grow your business into the future.

What are you currently doing to list and sell real estate? Probably more than you think. When is the last time you quantified your services? How are your services different from the services offered by your competition? How can you integrate technology solutions into your current methods of selling real estate?

To answer these questions, you must create a detailed list—a menu—of the services you currently provide to consumers. This will be discussed in detail in a later chapter.

GET CONNECTED

Most real estate professionals purchase technology in a haphazard way. They have no plan. What can today's real estate professional do to be positioned to become the **new real estate professional** and compete in this changing online environment? The answer is simple—get connected.

Getting connected is much more than going **online.** It is a mindset that begins with the purchase of a computer and the desire to interact with people via a new medium. For many, this will require a paradigm shift, a monumental cultural shift, and a major investment of time as well as money for "infrastructure."

Any real estate professional wishing to survive and thrive in the real estate industry of tomorrow—the "New Real Estate Industry"—must make a technology investment—and must begin to make that investment today. The real estate professional must make that investment within the structure of a defined plan, a **personal technology plan of action.** It's that or face a career change. As Dr. Denis Waitley says: *"It is online or the breadline."* Your technology investment consists of both money and time—money to purchase the technologies and time to learn how to use them. The good news is that the investment does not need to be made all at once. In fact, by the very nature of the changing technology and our human ability to learn and adapt, it can't be made all at once. The technology investment requires varying degrees of personal and monetary investment, over time, based on your budget, timetable, and commitment to success.

http://Commitment.RealTown.com

■ THE CONNECTED CONSUMER AND THE NEW REAL ESTATE PROFESSIONAL

The number of people using the Internet—each a connected consumer—is staggering. Estimates of online users vary into the millions, increasing exponentially. New consumers are younger and more efficient with each generation.

An increasing number of homebuyers today are using the Internet to research and gather information prior to contacting a real estate professional. As a result, they are further along in the homebuying process when they first approach a real estate professional. Your job as a real estate professional is to transform the mass of information into knowledge to help the homebuyer make a better buying decision. Because of the ease of searching for properties on the Internet, many homebuyers may begin their search well in advance of their actual time line to purchase. You must take time to develop online relationships, much the same as you take time to develop relationships with homeowners prior to listing a home for sale.

DEMANDS OF THE CONNECTED CONSUMER

Speed. Consumers want it now—look at the popularity of fast food and remote control. Make them wait and you could lose customers—the competition is just a click away. The new real estate professional immediately responds to **e-mail;** makes sure his or her **Web site** loads quickly, especially the property photos; and ensures the site is easy to navigate.

Convenience. Consumers will pay more for convenience. Convenience stores exist to fulfill this consumer demand, while charging higher prices. What are you doing in your real estate practice to bring convenience to your clients? The Internet offers unparalleled speed and convenience of communication.

■ TIP
Learn all you can about IDX (Internet Data Exchange) and VOW (Virtual Office Web Site) solutions available to you through your MLS or third-party vendors. Remember, Web sites with listing inventory are "stickier" than those without listing inventory.

Choice. Consumers want selection and choice. While it is true that too much choice can confuse (and a confused mind will say no), a variety of services and fee structures are appearing in the industry. How are you positioning yourself? Do you have the entire MLS inventory on your site? Have you outlined your menu of services?

http://IDXandVOW.RealTown.com

Value Added.   Consumers like to get MORE than they pay for; this is called *value added*. Real estate professionals provide value added services every day, but few take the time to reinforce this fact to their clients. Have you ever cleaned or painted a house for a client after a sale? Helped them move something like a refrigerator, an extra that wasn't in the listing agreement? That's value added.

Quality.   Are you willing to pay more for quality? Many people are.

Information.   This is the age of information! Consumers won't buy a toaster or a microwave without first buying a copy of *Consumer Guide*, let alone a piece of real estate. Make it quick (speed) and convenient for your clients to access plenty of (choice) information. Focus on your ability to gather, repackage, and distribute information.

Service.   Real estate is a service business. Once again—real estate is a service business. A certain portion of the population will always be willing to pay more for better service. Both the quality of your services and the quality of your environment fit into this consumer demand category.

Discounts.   Discounting fees is a legitimate way to compete. Everyone wants discounts. This demand is becoming more and more visible as consumers are able to use the Internet to do more of the legwork for themselves prior to beginning the search for a home. There will always be those willing to pay for full service, so brokers not willing to discount

> ■ **TIP**
> Highlight in your marketing materials any of the consumer demands listed above that you believe to be the hallmark of your services.

their fees and commissions must concentrate on other consumer demands. Remember that consumers will pay more for quality, service, and convenience. The nature of information dissemination via the Internet may have changed what has been an industry standard for years, the "Six Percent Commission." In many markets the average commission has decreased; to maintain a higher-than-average commission rate you will have to provide the consumer with other benefits.

ONLINE INFORMATION AVAILABLE TO THE CONNECTED CONSUMER

Inventory of Listings.   Today, homebuyers are able to access available listing inventory on national Web sites as well as on many broker, franchise, and licensee Web sites. As mentioned earlier, these new connected consumers have already seen much of what is available online before they contact a real estate professional. (They may know more about the market inventory than you do!) The online experience is becoming better and more realistic with **virtual tours.** Companies such as *VisualTour.com* provide panoramic photos of homes. As a result, the consumer is becoming more involved with all aspects of the real estate transaction. Having the information and knowing what to do with it are two different things—and this is where you can add value to the consumer.

Seller Listing Sites. "For sale by owner" sites are starting to emerge. Online auctions are getting off the ground as well. There are an increasing number of online commission rebate and referral programs. Before sellers list their homes they are asking real estate professionals during listing presentations to describe Internet marketing strategies, in addition to conventional marketing strategies.

Exposure sells real estate; the Internet is the ultimate exposure vehicle. Make sure you explain to prospective sellers all the things you will do to maximize the use of the Internet as you work to sell their home.

http://NewBusinessModels.RealTown.com

Online Loans. Loan information, application, and processing online are becoming more the norm than the exception. Lenders want to become the first point of contact in a real estate transaction and are gearing up for that role. Have you been to any online loan sites? It is important to explore and become conversant with some of the different online loan functionality available to both buyers and homeowners wishing to refinance. Being able to assist a buyer interested in procuring a loan online will set you apart from licensees who do not have this expertise.

How do you find out about online loan availability? Check out the Web sites of some of your favorite national lenders and see what they are offering. Radio and television stations are flooded with advertisements by online loan companies; take the time to examine them to learn of benefits and drawbacks.

The E-Transaction. The residential real estate transaction traditionally has been a lengthy process, filled with tightly controlled scheduling and passing back and forth of documents. Imagine, however, an online environment that enables all of the participants in a given transaction to communicate quickly, and pass documents, title reports, inspections, approvals, and authorizations between the buyer, seller, broker, and lender—without requiring any traveling or face-to-face scheduling. This is the new **e-transaction.** It is possible (if not probable) that we will see a significant speeding up of the typical real estate transaction as new efficiencies are applied via transaction networks and e-transaction platforms.

Buyers and sellers in the future will demand that their representative brokerages take advantage of these new efficiencies. Once again, technology offers the new real estate professionals the opportunity to stand out from competitors not willing to make the investment of time and money in new technology.

http://eTransaction.RealTown.com

CONSUMER DEMANDS AND EXPECTATIONS IN THE 21ST CENTURY

The successful 21st century real estate professional must be prepared to service the needs and expectations of an increasing number of information-empowered consumers. Many consumers are comfortable using the Internet to search for information and to shop online, thanks to experiences with companies such as *Amazon.com.*

■ UNDERSTANDING THE MIRACLE OF THE INTERNET

The Internet is the greatest meeting place in the world and the "network of networks." Everyone with access to the Internet has the ability to communicate with everyone else on the Internet and share information, ideas, business, and more. This creates a new channel of communication and a new marketing opportunity for the real estate professional—in fact, any professional seeking to develop stronger relationships with prospects, customers, clients, and referring agents (past, present, and future).

The Internet is fast becoming the preferred method of communication for a growing segment of the population. Real estate is a business of people, a business of networks and networking. Contact with people creates opportunity and the Internet allows users to reach more people with more information, more cost-effectively than ever before. Real estate information out of context is worthless, but real estate information in the context of the life of buyers and sellers is invaluable.

> **■ TIP**
> A simple differentiator is to ask everyone you meet for:
> 1. their e-mail address; and
> 2. their preferred method of communication— don't assume it is the telephone. Just asking this question will set you apart from your competition.

The skills required of real estate professionals will continue to change as technology changes the needs and expectations of the connected consumer. Even so, one thing is certain—the ability to use the Internet for communication and marketing will be essential for anyone expecting a successful career in real estate.

THE CREATION OF THE INTERNET

It is more important to know how to use the Internet than to know its complete history. Nevertheless, it is instructive to know something of its origins. Moreover, as a real estate professional you will meet potential customers and clients with an interest in the Internet and your ability to speak knowledgeably about its origin and history could prove to be of value to you. What follows is a summary of the origin of the Internet, arguably one of the most valuable technologies ever created.

In the Beginning. In 1957, President Dwight Eisenhower created two important programs: the Interstate Highway System and the Advanced Research Projects Agency, or ARPA. Both programs were established in response to the general threat of the Soviet Union, particularly in light of the successful launching of its **Sputnik** spacecraft. ARPA developed **ARPANET,** the forerunner of the Internet.

Information superhighway is a buzzword from a speech by then Vice President Al Gore that refers to the Clinton/Gore administration's plan to deregulate communication services and widen the scope of the Internet by opening carriers (such as television cable) to data communication. The Internet or "The Net" is not a single network; rather, it is a group of thousands of individual networks that have chosen to allow traffic to pass among them using a common protocol.

The **World Wide Web (WWW)** is a subset of the Internet. It allows the retrieval and use of text, graphics, audio, and video (multimedia) from remote locations, providing information on most every subject imaginable and based on **point-and-click** technology.

The Web was first conceived in 1989 by Tim Berners-Lee of CERN (The European Laboratory for Particle Physics).

The Web is only a part of the Internet—the graphical, browser-viewed, point-and-click part of the Internet. While the Internet has been around since the late 1960s, the World Wide Web began its growth in popularity and use in the early 1990s with the commercialization of the **browser** (software that allows you to "surf" the Web).

Chapter Links:
http://Commitment.RealTown.com
http://IDXandVOW.RealTown.com
http://NewBusinessModels.RealTown.com
http://eTransaction.RealTown.com

■ REVIEW QUESTIONS

1. Can technology be integrated selectively into your business or must you be ready to implement the full scope of real estate-related technologies to generate benefits?

   Answer: As with real estate in general, when it comes to the use of technology, "it's the little things that make a difference." Technology is not an all or nothing proposition. As you learn new technologies or technology related skills, it is important to put them to work immediately and they will, in time, have an impact on your business and your success.

2. (T/F) When one speaks of the Internet, one is referring specifically to what is also known as the World Wide Web (WWW).

   Answer: False.

   The World Wide Web is only a part of the Internet—the graphical, browser-viewed, point-and-click part of the Internet. While the Internet has been around since the late 1960s, the World Wide Web began its growth in popularity and use in the early 1990s with the commercialization of the browser (software that allows you to "surf" the Web).

3. What are five of the eight stated consumer demands?

    Answer: Speed/Convenience/Choice/Value Added/ Discounts/Quality/Service/Information

Chapter Two

How the Internet Works
Domain Names and Hosting

You cannot change your destiny overnight, but you can change your direction in this moment.
DENIS WAITLEY
http://Motivation.RealTown.com

■ DOMAIN NAME SYSTEM (DNS)—
MATCHING NAMES WITH NUMBERS

The first step to understanding how the Internet works is to become clear about the **Domain Name System (DNS)** and how domain names can be used in your business.

The Domain Name System is very complicated. As a real estate professional, you don't need to know how DNS works, it just needs to work for you. Do know this—however, if DNS fails to work, Web sites cannot be located and e-mail cannot be delivered. Failure of DNS could be devastating to your Internet marketing and online communication endeavors.

The Domain Name System (DNS) is a distributed domain directory service. It directs Web site requests and/or e-mail sent to a specific domain to the appropriate Internet location. Think of it as the automated 411 of the Internet (making the connection for you), which contains a directory (like the phone book) copied to different locations (called root servers) around the world and updated regularly.

A **DNS server** is a computer running DNS software. The most popular DNS program is BIND (Berkeley Internet Name Domain) developed at the University of California at Berkeley.

11

DOMAIN NAMES

A **domain name** is a unique Internet identifier. It allows computers connected to the Internet to locate other computers connected to the Internet quickly and easily by using a name instead of a series of numbers. Without domain names, Internet users would have to type in a string of numbers each time they wanted to access information or communicate with another computer through the Internet.

When you want someone to locate or communicate with you on the Internet (in a virtual world), you give them your domain name just as you would give someone your telephone number or street address to locate or communicate with you in the physical world. People find it much easier to remember *InternetCrusade.com* than to remember InternetCrusade's Internet Protocol (IP) address, which is 209.251.24.84.

A domain name is simply a language-based address system (i.e., *InternetCrusade.com)* in which each name, word, or series of words or initials refers to a specific number-based address or location on the Internet (i.e., 209.251.24.84).

Domain Name Conventions. Domain names may be up to 67 characters in length, including the **TLD** (63 characters plus .com, .net, .org). Allowable characters are letters, numbers, and dashes (-). Dashes are not allowed at the beginning or the end of a domain. Exclamation marks, underscores, and blank spaces are not permitted. Spaces are not allowed between words—so, to distinguish one word from another when using your domain in a marketing setting, use upper and lower case. Once again, the little things make a difference.

The Internet is not case sensitive when it comes to e-mail and Web site addresses **(URLs).** Therefore using upper and lower case in printed marketing materials—which makes e-mail and Web site addresses easier to read—is permissible.

Here are some examples of using upper and lower case:

forbesbest.com
ForbesBest.com
epronar.com
eProNAR.com

You will not find Jim's Head at *www.jimshead.com;* you will, however, find Jim Shead! It is not necessary to type capitals, but when marketing your domain, capitals help your domain stand out and become easier to read.

Here are more examples of using upper and lower case:

generhodes.coom
GeneRhodes.com
williamsteam.com
WilliamsTeam.com

Although you may change professions or switch companies, one constant that helps to identify you is your personal name. When you attempt to register your domain name, first try to register your last name (*Smith.com*); if that is taken, then your first and last name (*Janie-Smith.com*); and, if that is taken, then perhaps insert a dash between the first and last name (*Janie-Smith.com*). You might want to try something like *AlaskaBob.com;* or *CallJohn.com;* or *SellKona.com* or *NewYork-Homes.com.* Be creative. If you are known by a different business name, or as a team, choose a domain that mirrors your offline marketing and branding efforts. When you go to sell your company one day, a creative domain name may make it more marketable.

■ DOMAIN LEVELS

TOP LEVEL DOMAINS (TLD)

The first level of domain names is referred to as a Top Level Domain or TLD. The six most common TLDs are .com, .net, .org, .edu, .gov, and .mil. Additional TLDs approved in 2000 are .biz, .pro, .name, .info, .coop, .museum, and .aero.

The internationally recognized governing body for TLDs is the Internet Corporation for Assigned Names and Numbers, located on the Internet at *http://ICANN.org.*

The most well-known and widely used TLD is .com. Billions of dollars have been spent branding the .com TLD into the hearts and souls of the consuming public. Just as the 800 number is the most desired and well-known of the toll-free telephone numbers, .com is the most desired and most remembered of the TLDs. The TLD .net is a poor second choice.

If you wanted a toll-free number for your business and were given the option of 800, 888, 877, or 866, you would probably opt for 800 as it remains the most recognized of the toll-free numbers. Often, when one is given an 888 or other toll-free number, that person instinctively dials 800, even while looking at a business card that indicates the number is 888. This same sort of thing can occur when Internet users are typing a domain name into their browser to view a Web site—often people will instinctively insert the .com suffix. For example, you may want to get in touch with the IRS and instinctively type in *www.IRS.com*. What you'll get is a company promoting accounting services (IRS can be found at *www.IRS.gov*). You wouldn't want a customer going to your competitor's Web site because you chose an uncommon TLD.

As the Internet Corporation for Assigned Names and Numbers (ICANN) continues to approve new TLDs for the Internet, this could change, but right now .com is king.

SECOND LEVEL DOMAIN (SLD)

Care and maintenance of Top Level Domains are assigned to an official registry; each TLD has its own registry. The registry maintains the Root Servers and issues rights to **Second Level Domains (SLDs),** names such as *InternetCrusade.com, REALTOR.com, YourName.com*, etc., to the public, organizations, and government, usually for a fee, through companies known as **registrars** (and their resellers). Regardless of which **registrar** an individual may use to register a domain, the registration goes into the registry for that particular TLD.

In the case of some TLDs, like .gov, there are restrictions on who can register an SLD of that top level domain type. For example, not just anyone can register a .mil, .edu, or .gov domain. For .mil, only the military qualifies and the .mil registry will not accept .mil registrations unless its qualifying parameters are met. The same is true with .edu for qualified educational institutions and .gov for government institutions.

If you do not own a Second Level Domain, purchasing one should be the first step on your technology "to do" list. Just owning a second level domain is a differentiator—and remember, in the "me too" business of real estate, you want to differentiate yourself—to make yourself unique—from your competition. While there are literally hundreds of companies from which you can purchase

■ TIP

At the very least you should attempt to own YourLastName.com, YourFirstNameLast Name.com, or YourCompany.com. Buy it now before someone else does—it may already be too late.

Second Level Domains, InternetCrusade became the exclusive domain partner of the National Association of REALTORS® in 2000 and you can register Second Level Domains at *http://Dearborn.RealTown.com.*

■ DOMAIN REGISTRATION

Why register a domain name now? Because it might not be available tomorrow!

Domain names are issued on a first-come, first-served basis and may be registered for periods of up to ten years. Once a name is taken, it is unavailable unless the current owner wants to sell it to you, usually for a hefty fee. Domain names are

> **■ TIP**
> Do not purchase the domain name of a company or entity that is trademarked.

unique. Only one person or entity can hold a license for a particular domain. As a general rule, you should not register a domain containing someone else's federally registered trademark; otherwise you may be challenged by the trademark owner and risk losing the domain, and be liable for monetary damages under the federal Anti-cybersquatting Consumer Protection Act (ACPA).

A domain name is the foundation of an Internet identity. Having an Internet address is mandatory in today's real estate business—as important as having a phone number. Whether you decide to use a domain now or later, once you have it registered no one else can use your domain name (for the duration of the domain license period you purchased, to a maximum of ten years unless extended). The smart business decision is to register your name and/or company name without delay so that the domain(s) will be available when needed.

There are hundreds of Web sites real estate professionals can use for domain registration. Keep in mind that different companies offer different levels of customer and follow-up service with registration. Make sure you choose a company that has been in the domain and e-mail business for at least five years and a company that provides a high level of customer service. Don't be "penny wise and pound foolish" in the handling of your domain. Your choice of registrars has a direct impact on your marketing and communication on the Internet.

When registering a Second Level Domain, make sure you:

- are the owner (**registrant** or organization)—you can check to see if you are the listed registrant of your domain by going to *http://Domains.RealTown.com* and clicking on the button that says "Whois", which is generic Internet terminology for the Directories of TLDs;
- receive a **registry key** or equivalent administrative control at the time of registration;
- purchase a multiyear license (up to ten years) to minimize the possibility that you might forget to renew, thus losing all the marketing investment you have in your domain name, including the lost business that would result from future undelivered e-mail sent to your old domain;
- use a registration system that processes in real time so no one beats you to the registry at the last minute and registers the same domain you were intending to register. Domains are registered on a first-come, first-served basis. In the event of a dispute over a domain containing a previously federally registered trademark, the trademark owner generally would prevail; (see *http:// Domain Disputes.Realtown.com*) and
- secure your Internet identity today. Buy your domain name now; you can "park" the domain until you decide to use it for e-mail or a Web site. Parking will secure the name for you (for the period of time you purchased the domain name, one to ten years). To use your domain, it must be hosted on a **domain name server** (both a primary and secondary domain name server), which can then direct traffic to your e-mail account and Web site.

Remember, you don't need to have a Web site or an e-mail account to acquire your domain name. You may register domains for periods of up to ten years. The registration process can be handled online in a matter of minutes, with your receiving an e-mail notice that includes your **registry key number.** This number will allow you to make certain online changes to the registration information, even the location of your DNS servers. You are the owner and you are in control—for as long as your license is owned and renewed. Make sure you register your domain with a company (registrar) that provides you with a registry key and a Web interface to use it.

■ DOMAIN NAMES AND A PERMANENT E-MAIL ADDRESS

Your e-mail address is an asset of your business, and it is an asset you invest in every time you give out a business card or marketing piece that includes your e-mail address. You are teaching the world that if they want to reach you by e-mail, they should send it to that e-mail address. It is for this reason that you want to own your e-mail address and be able to take it with you from **Internet Service Provider (ISP)** to ISP or from one real estate company to another.

If you don't have your own domain, then more than likely, your e-mail address is a user name at the domain of your ISP. Using Janie123@AOL.com as our example, Janie123 is the user name and AOL.com is the domain name. Every time Janie uses this address, she is promoting AOL.com.

Doesn't it make better sense to promote your own Internet identity rather than that of the ISP? If you are like most real estate professionals, your name plays a key part in your marketing efforts. If you are going to do business on the Internet, you must create an Internet presence. To do this, you must obtain your own domain name. Some real estate professionals use their name in the selection of their domain. This makes sense as your name is your brand and your brand is your name. The secret to success in real estate marketing is putting your name in front of people over and over again. Others use a slogan or geographic location. It is not so much what you choose, but that you choose, that is important. Choose to use a domain name that is branded to you.

Every business card you give out, every ad you run, every brochure you distribute with an e-mail address on it is an investment in that e-mail address that will accrue to the owner of the e-mail address. If you are using an e-mail address with any domain other than one you own, you are making a serious mistake. **A significant benefit of owning your own domain is a permanent e-mail address.** Change ISPs as often as you want—the permanent address does not change.

If Janie acquires the domain name *JanieSmith.com,* her permanent e-mail address can be Janie@JanieSmith.com and the new World Wide Web address of her Web site now becomes *http://JanieSmith.com.*

Note the consistency that her domain name gives to her e-mail address and her Web site address. Consistency is a prime ingredient of your Internet marketing plan.

E-MAIL FORWARDING

With **e-mail forwarding,** e-mail addressed to you at your branded domain name is sent to your domain host's server. From there it is automatically redirected to your mailbox account, which more than likely is being provided by your current internet service provider (ISP) as part of the price of your connectivity package. You will encounter the term **POP,** which stands for post office protocol and just indicates that it is an Internet e-mail account.

The beauty of e-mail forwarding is that you can change your ISP (or real estate brokerage) at any time and it will have no effect on your permanent e-mail or Web address. If you want to switch to a faster or less expensive Internet access service, you will not have to worry about changing business cards and stationery to reflect a new e-mail address and Web site address. Only YOU will know about the change.

E-mail forwarding is an entry level e-mail service but all that one needs to get started with a permanent e-mail address. As you learn more about the power of e-mail, you may opt for more sophisticated e-mail services from an e-mail host.

Let's go back to our example—if Janie changes her ISP from *AOL.com* to *Earthlink.net,* she simply instructs her domain host (either by e-mail or on a Web interface) to reprogram their server to send her e-mail to her new account at Earthlink. This is all behind the scenes;

> **■ TIP**
> Don't wait to establish a permanent e-mail address. Do it now at http://Dearborn.RealTown.com

her business cards remain unchanged—they still accurately read Janie@JanieSmith.com for her e-mail address and *http://JanieSmith.com* for her Web site address. There is no need to send out a mass mailing to inform people to change her e-mail and Web site address. This is what we mean by a permanent Internet identity. It is simple—and effective.

As previously mentioned, once you own a Second Level Domain, you will use it for e-mail and your Web site. You will also be able to create **Third Level Domains** to provide a unique and intuitive navigational structure for your Web site. This structure can result in increased Web site traffic—for example, Janie could direct prospects to her online listings with the Third Level Domain:

FeaturedProperties.JanieSmith.com
.com = top level
JanieSmith = second level
FeaturedProperties = third level

■ WEB FORWARDING (POINTING)

Web forwarding (pointing) is the functionality that allows you (through your domain host) to point your domain to your Web site. You can acquire as many domains as you wish and have them all directed (pointed) to your Web site.

POINTER DOMAINS

It is common practice for successful real estate professionals to use more than one domain to drive traffic, both intentional and unintentional, to their Web site. In addition, e-mail sent to many different domains can all be delivered to the same e-mail account.

Here are several examples of **pointer domains:**

- Common misspelling of your name (domain)—If someone misspells your name, do you still want to receive e-mail from them and would you still like for them to visit your Web site? Dr. Denis Waitley registered the domains *DenisWaitley.com* and *DennisWaitley.com.*
- Geographic names such as *SanDiegoRealEstate.com*—Many people search for properties by location.
- Marketing names such as *YourRealEstateBroker.com*—Use a domain that ties in with your current marketing themes.
- Random names to capture wandering Web surfing eyeballs—Use name such as:
  - *http://ParisInTheSpring.com*
  - *http://StubbornAsAMule.com*
  - *http://FrequentlyAskedQuestions.com*
  - *http://RoyalHawaiian.com*
  - *http://InternetBusinessAdvisors.com*
  - *http://IsThereaDoctorIntheHouse.com*
  - *http://ItIsEasyWhenYouKnowHow.com*
  . . . which all point to the InternetCrusade Web site.

Owning and pointing multiple domains to the main Web site is one way of ensuring that the visitor who is trying to find information finds you. They will find you even if they do not always spell your name correctly or do not usually search by your name (e.g., search for homes in Pittsburgh instead of searching for *JanieSmith.com*). They will find you because you have set up paths via pointer domains for them to end up at your main domain. Making all pointer domains link to your main (branded) domain will help ensure that Web surfers see your name every time—even when they did not know your name when they started their search.

■ DOMAIN NAMES IN COMMUNICATION AND MARKETING

For marketing purposes, branding is defined as the ongoing exposure of a product, service, or company name to an audience that results in the recognition of the product, service, company when the brand is seen or heard. When you think of Coca-Cola, Tide, and Kodak, you can immediately recall the products or services they represent. That is high-level brand name recognition, achieved through consistent, long-term exposure and investment of marketing dollars over long periods of time.

Most real estate professionals are independent contractors. They market both the companies they work for and also themselves (their name). They do this on all their marketing materials—business cards, flyers, signs, calendars, vehicle plates, magnets, pens, flyswatters, and other items real estate professionals are known for giving away. What name do you want the homeowners in your farm area to think about when they hear the words real estate? How about yours? Most successful real estate professionals today promote their names everywhere they can (your name is your brand, your brand is your name). How much money have you spent over the years getting your brand (your name) out into the public? Add it all up and, depending on how long you have been in the business, it can be a considerable amount.

MAKING A NAME FOR YOURSELF ON THE INTERNET

To take your brand to the Internet, you should become *Your-Brand.com*. This requires the purchase of your own Second Level Domain. That is, for example, InternetCrusade in *www.Internet Crusade.com*. Marketing yourself on the Internet begins with this very simple step.

If you plan to use the federally registered trademark REALTOR® in a domain, make sure you follow the National Association of REALTORS® (NAR) terms of use. You would not want to spend money on a domain name that you are ultimately told (by NAR) you may not use. Use by an individual or a company of the term REALTOR® with name is permitted if they are members, but using REALTOR® with a geographic location or descriptive term is prohibited (REALTOR® associations can obtain authorization). Also, be sure to follow the rules of the franchisor if you are using the franchise name in your domain.

Example of misuse: *SanDiegoREALTOR.com*
Example of misuse: *YourREALTOR4Life.com*
Example of misuse: *DallasREALTOR@AOL.com*

Example of proper use: *JohnREALTOR.com*
Example of proper use: *MikeBarnettREALTOR.com*
Example of proper use: *REALTORSaulKlein.com*

It is not necessary to capitalize the word REALTOR® nor to use the registered trademark as reference to the word REALTOR® in your domain name. It has become an industry standard to use lower cases when accessing Web domains and thus the National Association of REALTORS® has given exceptions to these two rules. Before selecting a domain that uses the REALTOR® mark, go to *http://UseOfREALTORina Domain.RealTown.com* to review the current rules.

Use your domain for both your e-mail address and your Web address. Have a consistent Internet marketing presence.

For example:
Web Address: *http://YourName.com*
E-mail Address: You@YourName.com

■ DOMAIN NAME RENEWAL AND TRANSFER

Many companies today are sending both e-mail and **snail mail** to domain owners telling them that their domain is about to expire and to renew the domain with that company. Often these are schemes to transfer your domain from your current domain host and in many cases to take your money without renewing your domain. Just because you get a notice that your domain is due to expire does not necessarily mean that it *is* going to expire. Make sure you know when your domain expires. If you do not know, go to *http://Domains.RealTown.com* and conduct a search at the Whois tab.

FAILURE TO RENEW

When you own a domain, you own the exclusive rights to that domain for the entire license period. If you fail to renew by the expiration date, you might find that someone else has acquired the domain. This could have disastrous consequences if you have Web and e-mail tied to that domain. More than one real estate professional has failed to renew the ownership of a domain, only to find that the domain was subsequently purchased by a pornography company and pointed to a pornography Web site.

In some cases, you may decide to transfer the domain registration to another registrar. Here, in question and answer format, are some key points about domain renewals and transfers.

DOMAIN RENEWAL FREQUENTLY ASKED QUESTIONS (FAQS)

Q: Do I have to wait until the stated expiration date before renewing my domain name?

A: You don't have to wait for your domain name registration to expire before renewing it. In fact, it is a good idea to extend the term well before the expiration date. Why worry about letting the expiration date pass by because you were too busy and it slipped your mind? The term you choose for renewal will be added to your existing term no matter when you renew.

Q: Will I be notified in advance of the expiration date of any domains I may have purchased?

A: That depends on which registrar you used and whether you are listed as the registrant and the administrative contact—and whether your contact information is current. This illustrates the importance of using a registrar who offers you the tools to maintain your domain contact information through a simple Web interface.

Q: How long can I extend the registration of my domain name?

A: You can extend the registration for up to another nine years (cannot exceed ten years). You simply add time to your existing registration term—and you can do this at any time. The cost per year decreases for the longer-term extensions such as five and nine years. More important, especially if the domain name is an integral part of your Internet identity, you don't have to worry each year about losing this prized asset and having someone else claim it.

Q: What happens if I fail to take action before the expiration date?

A: Depending on the Registrar, there may be a short grace period for you to renew the registration term before the name is released back to the pool of available names and anyone else can pick it up. Loss of domain name will terminate related services such as e-mail and Web forwarding. Don't risk any changes in the unofficial grace period—renew your domain name well in advance.

Q: How do I find out the expiration dates of any of my domains?

A: Check in the Whois for domain contact information including expiration date. Go to *http://Domains.RealTown.com* and click on the Whois tab. Insert your domain name including the extension (such as .com or .org).

DOMAIN TRANSFER FAQS

Q: What is a domain name transfer of registrar?

A: Transferring means changing the registrar, the entity that registers domain names for individuals and organizations. If you have domains that were registered with other registrars such as Network Solutions, you do not have to renew your domain with them. You can transfer the domain to any registrar at any time. Some registrars offer better service than others. Transfer needs to be done before the domain name expires. (Allow several weeks.) Transferring a domain name does not mean transfer of ownership or changing the hosting company. If you want to transfer your domain name to a hosting company, please refer to the section below entitled "How do I transfer my domain to my hosting company?"

Q: Will transferring domain name registrars change my information?

A: No, all existing information in your domain record will remain the same. The transfer process does not change your name servers; thus your e-mail and Web sites will not be affected by the move to transfer registrars.

Q: Are there any restrictions on making the transfer?

A: In most cases, the transfer is a simple process that can be handled online. The following are some of the more exceptional situations that can prevent or delay a transfer:

1. The domain has already expired.
2. The domain will expire within the next several weeks. In this event, your best step is to return to the existing registrar and renew so you don't risk losing the domain. Then transfer to your desired registrar.
3. The domain was registered within the last 60 days. Under current rules, wait until the 60 days have passed and then proceed with the transfer.
4. You don't have access to the current administrative contact (the designated contact person)—note that the administrative contact's approval via e-mail is required. If your domain's administrative contact e-mail address is not valid anymore, you will not receive the important e-mail confirmation message—you should first update the e-mail address with your current registrar, and then apply for transfer. This is the most common reason that transfer failures occur. You can use the Whois tab at *http://Domains.RealTown.com* to find out the current administrative contact e-mail address in your domain record. It will also show you the date the domain was registered, the date it expires, and the administrative contact e-mail address.

Q: Are there any transfer fees? What is my cost?

A: Typically, there is no transfer fee. The only amount you will be charged is approximately $25 for a one-year registration. This registration will add one year to the current expiration date of the domain no matter how early you do the transfer. You might want to consider extending the term for five or nine years so you won't have to keep thinking about missing one of the annual renewals.

Q: What are the steps in the transfer of registrar process?

A: 1. The very first step is to check the Whois tab to ascertain if your current e-mail address is reflected in the administrative contact section. If it is not, then immediately contact the registrar to change the administrative contact e-mail address so that you will be able to authenticate the confirmation e-mail that is sent to that address.

2. Next, submit a transfer request to your current registrar. A confirmation e-mail will be sent back to the administrative contact e-mail address of record. Follow the instructions sent in that e-mail to indicate your approval and complete it within four days.

3. The approval from you will be sent to the current, or "losing," registrar for their approval. They must approve or reject (normally within seven days). They usually don't wait that long. Based on the $25 (approximately) registration fee, your domain will be renewed for one year and the new expiration date will be one year from the last expiration date.

Q: How do I transfer my domain to my hosting company?

A: Transferring to a hosting company is not the same as transferring from a registrar or transferring ownership. All you need to do is to change the name servers of your domain to the name servers of your hosting company. This change can take place at any time online if your registrar provides you with a domain manager tool.

> **■ TIP**
> If e-mail and Web services are already connected to your domain, be sure to use an experienced domain host to limit any possible interruption in e-mail and Web service during the transfer.

Q: My current administrative contact e-mail is wrong. How can I submit a transfer request?

A: Contact your current registrar and have the registrar correct your administrative contact e-mail address. Before submitting the transfer request, use the Whois search to make sure the updated e-mail address appears in your domain record. Even after your registrar says it is updated, it can take a few days for the new e-mail address to appear in the domain record.

Q: What is a Domain Management System?

A: It is an enhanced Web tool that enables you to log in and access your registered domain information for maintenance, update, and editing purposes. The Domain Management System becomes available for use immediately after your registration and receipt of your unique registry key.

Chapter Links:
http://Dearborn.RealTown.com
http://Domains.RealTown.com
http://UseOfREALTORinADomain.RealTown.com
http://DomainDisputes.RealTown.com

■ REVIEW QUESTIONS

1. What is the Domain Name System?

   Answer: The Domain Name System (DNS) is a distributed domain directory service. It directs Web site requests and/or e-mail sent to a specific domain to the appropriate Internet location. Think of it as the automated 411 of the Internet (making the connection for you), which contains a directory (like the phone book), copied to different locations (**root servers**) around the world and updated regularly.

2. Why is DNS important?

   Answer: If DNS fails to work, Web sites cannot be located and e-mail cannot be delivered. Failure of DNS could be devastating to your Internet marketing and online communication endeavors.

3. Why is it important not to change one's e-mail address? Why is it important to have a permanent e-mail address?

    Answer: Your e-mail address is an asset of your business and it is an asset you invest in every time you give out a business card or marketing piece that includes your e-mail address. You are teaching the world that if they want to reach you by e-mail, they should send it to that e-mail address. It is for this reason that you want to own your e-mail address and be able to take it with you from ISP to ISP or from one real estate company to another.

4. What is required to have a permanent e-mail address?

    Answer: You must have your own domain and at the very minimum, an e-mail forwarding account.

Three Types of Internet Hosting

A problem defined is half solved.
DENIS WAITLEY
http://Motivation.RealTown.com

Internet hosting comprises a broad body of knowledge. Not all technology companies have the same level of expertise when it comes to the Internet, just as not all real estate licensees have the same level of real estate expertise.

Hosting is the allowance of storage space and resources on Internet servers. For most people, it is less expensive to rent space on someone else's Internet **server** than to own and maintain an Internet server of one's own.

There are three types of Internet hosting:

1. Domain Hosting
2. E-mail Hosting
3. Web Site Hosting

When most people hear the word *hosting* in the context of the Internet, their first thought is Web site hosting. Many believe this to be the only type of hosting. In fact, Web (site) hosting (providing storage space for files retrievable through the use of the Internet) is only one aspect of Internet hosting; all three types are essential to establishing and maintaining a presence on the Internet. Each type of hosting has its own value and importance. The types of hosting are not necessarily tied to one another; different vendors can provide each type of hosting, or the same vendor can provide all three types of hosting. Consider the following:

- Your domain host does not need to be the company that hosts your Web site or your e-mail.
- Your e-mail host does not need to be the company that hosts your domain and your Web site.
- Your Web site host does not need to be the company that hosts your domain or your e-mail.

■ DOMAIN HOSTING

Your domain host should offer you the ability to point any request to your domain to any Web site you indicate as well as direct your e-mail to any e-mail account you may have established with any vendor.

The first level of the domain name—the TLD—usually indicates the type of entity that owns the domain: (.com) commercial, (.mil) military, (.edu) educational, (.gov) government, and more, as explained previously.

When a Second Level Domain is registered (YourName.com), the registry requires the registrant (owner) to provide two Domain Name Servers (DNS) (primary and secondary) for each domain. If you don't own your own DNS when you register a domain name (and most of us do not), you may use the services of someone who does, by providing their DNS numbers to the registry as the primary and secondary address for your domain. This entity is your domain host.

Your domain host should make sure that Web requests to your domain will easily locate your Web site, whether or not the person attempting to find your site typed "www" into the **browser** address box. Other things might prevent a "call" from reaching its desired destination, but not the inclusion or exclusion

> ## ■ TIP
> Make sure your domain host has located its DNS servers in two different locations. How do you know? Ask your host.

of the "www." Be sure to ask your domain host to make the appropriate "Cname" entry so that your Web site can be accessed with or without using the "www."

■ E-MAIL HOSTING

When discussing e-mail (which we will do in greater detail in a later chapter), it is instructional to consider two sides to e-mail—client side and server side. The client side is the software that is resident on your computer, complete with all the **functionality** your software provides. Examples of client side e-mail software are Microsoft's Outlook Express, Outlook, and Eudora.

Server side is once again software, but this time it resides on an Internet server, typically that of your Internet Service Provider (ISP). As with all software, server side e-mail software can do many things and has very useful functionality for the new real estate professionals.

An e-mail host is the entity that provides you with **virtual post office** services. Many real estate professionals receive some of the basic post office services, such as limited mailbox accounts, as part of a monthly ISP fee.

Nearly every hosting company will promote its services on an offering site or an ad. Read that information carefully, looking for the specific information noted below. In the event the information is not detailed or clear, you must ask the company for answers. Normally, each hosting company's Web site will have a section titled "Contact Us" or some similar communication instruction. It will often give you a list of e-mail addresses and phone numbers to call to get your answers. Don't assume that you will get all services with all host offerings. You must ask to be certain.

VIRTUAL POST OFFICE FUNCTIONALITY— E-MAIL PROTOCOL

The e-mail **protocols** to be familiar with are the **POP account**—specifically POP3—and **IMAP,** defined below.

POP3 Account. While the general concept of e-mail is that it is byte size and takes up no space, the fact is that it uses cyber resources (servers, licenses, connectivity, etc). More and more e-mail is arriving with **attachments** such as photo and WAV (audio) files, which require server storage (albeit temporary), and increase the need for additional resources. POP3 account services include the physical space where e-mail resides (on the Internet server of the e-mail host) until **downloaded**—it is your electronic mailbox. Real estate professionals need to think about the following:

- The size restrictions on POP3 accounts and the cost for additional space—The average POP3 account limit with ISPs is 3 to 8 MB **(megabytes)**.

- Size limitations on attachments—Some e-mail hosts restrict the size of any given incoming or outgoing message. This can be as small as 1 MB, including attachments. Make sure that your e-mail host allows files large enough to include pictures and data tables.
- What occurs when your account goes over the limit—Does the account reject any e-mail sent to the account if the maximum has been reached and does it notify the sender that the message was rejected? Have you ever received a reply message that said ". . . box over quota?"
- Whether there are restrictions on the number of messages you can send out at one time—Some anti-**spam** measures that ISPs employ could create obstacles for your mass e-mail campaigns.

POP3 Account Features. POP3 account features include the following:

- **Vacation message**—which can be used as an auto reply confirmation of receipt of e-mail
- Web controls—which enable you to make changes to your e-mail account on a Web site from any computer with access to the Internet
- **Web Mail**—which allows you access to your POP3 account mail from any computer connected to the Internet, via a password-protected Web site
- Unlimited e-mail addressing—which enables you to create e-mail addresses on the fly, and can be used for ad tracking and control
- E-mail forwarding—which redirects e-mail sent to your domain to any mail box (POP3 account or any e-mail-enabled appliance, such as a pager, cellular phone, or wireless **handheld device**)

Post Office Protocol (POP) works best when one has only a single computer where messages are downloaded and then deleted from the mail server. This mode of access is not compatible with access from multiple computers as it tends to sprinkle messages across all computers used for mail access (although you can activate the "leave a copy of mail on server" setting, allowing you to maintain all files on one master computer).

With POP, unless all of those machines share a common file system, the **offline** mode of access that POP was designed to support effectively ties the user to one computer for message storage and manipulation.

INTERNET MESSAGE ACCESS PROTOCOL (IMAP)

IMAP is a method of accessing e-mail or bulletin board messages that are kept on a mail server. It allows a client e-mail program to access remote message stores as if they were local. For example, e-mail stored on an IMAP server can be manipulated from a **desktop computer** at home, a workstation at the office, and a notebook computer while traveling, without the need to transfer messages or files back and forth between these computers.

IMAP's ability to access messages (both new and saved) from more than one computer has become extremely important with the increased reliance on electronic messaging and use of multiple computers.

> ■ **TIP**
> Know the features and limitations of your e-mail account. Whom do you ask? Your e-mail host.

WEB HOSTING

Web hosting companies rent storage space (usually measured in megabytes or **gigabytes**) on their Internet servers for your Web page files. Their fees are usually based on a combination of space and **bandwidth** or **throughput.**

Web hosting companies can provide many types of services, including Web site management tools. These specialized tools can give you useful Web site statistics, not just a counter seen on many Web sites. Web statistics software is thorough and powerful when used, and it is inexpensive. It will help you gauge the effectiveness of your Internet marketing efforts by providing information such as:

- page views per day, week, month, and year;
- number of people on the site at any point in time;
- referring sites;
- page where viewers enter site;
- page where viewers exit site; and
- operating system and browser information of visitors to the site.

Real estate professionals have varying needs for Web hosting space and bandwidth, based on their overall marketing plan and their marketing budget. There are many choices of services. Do not spend any money on a Web site until you have completed your **technology plan of action** and know what, why, where, when, how, who, and how much. We'll discuss this in later chapters.

■ HOSTING FACILITIES

Common to all three types of hosting is the need for a secure facility (preferably a **hardened data center**).

How long could you stay in business if your Web site were not visible to the public, or, more immediately, if your e-mail stopped working? If your communication and marketing ability are important to you, the physical location and fail-safes of your Internet hosts should be a high priority. Servers accessing the Internet can be located in office buildings and even garages. If you are using your domain, e-mail, and the Web in your business, and your business is more than a hobby to you, you will want the security and services provided by a hardened data center, services such as:

- security cameras;
- security officers;
- redundant power systems—36-hour full power generator—important in the era of rolling blackouts;
- redundant Internet connections;
- **24/7/365** monitoring and maintenance where servers are **pinged** frequently; and
- HVAC and fire protection, allowing for the smothering of a fire by forcing the oxygen out of the room as opposed to dowsing everything (including the servers) with high pressure blasts of water.

■ TIP

1. If you don't own a domain, purchase one.
2. Review your current e-mail situation. If you are using any e-mail address other than an e-mail address of a domain you own, begin the process of changing e-mail addresses after reading the next chapter.
3. If you own your domain, make sure your Web site can be located with or without typing "www" into the browser.
4. Are you receiving e-mail at more than one location? If yes, explore the benefits of IMAP.

For further detailed information on hosting, see the article at *http://GuideToHosting.RealTown.com*.

Chapter Links:
http://GuideToHosting.RealTown.com

■ REVIEW QUESTIONS

1. What are the three types of hosting?

   Answer:

   Domain Hosting
   E-mail Hosting
   Web Site Hosting

2. Is it required that your Web site host also host your domain?

   Answer: It is certainly not an Internet requirement, although it may be a company requirement of the marginal Web hosting companies. Remember, your domain host does not need to be the company that hosts your Web site or your e-mail, your e-mail host does not need to be the company that hosts your domain and your Web site, and your Web site host does not need to be the company that hosts your domain or your e-mail.

3. What are the two sides of e-mail?

   Answer:

   Client Side: Software on your computer
   Server Side: Services available through a hosting company or ISP

Chapter Four

Connecting to the Internet

There never was a winner, who wasn't a beginner.
DENIS WAITLEY
http://Motivation.RealTown.com

The Internet is a tool made for the real estate business. The Internet is people networking with people, allowing information to be transferred almost instantaneously (at the push of a button, at the speed of light). As real estate is an information-dependent "people business," the transfer of information in a fast and cost-effective manner is key to the success of the real estate professional today, and will be even more so in the future.

Connecting to the Internet can be a maze of different choices. Which service is the best? What should you pay? What do you really need? What services should you expect?

You gain access to the Internet and Internet communications (e-mail, **ftp, Instant Messaging (IM),** etc.) through companies referred to as Internet Service Providers (ISPs). The two basic methods of access are referred to as **dial-up,** which is telephone line access (POTS for Plain Old Telephone Service) and **broadband,** which includes **DSL, cable, corporate networks** such as T1 and T3, and a few others.

■ INTERNET SERVICE PROVIDERS (ISPs)

An ISP is a company that provides individuals and businesses with access to the Internet, often by purchasing access from larger carriers and then reselling it. Once you have access to the Internet, you will need a browser (such as Microsoft's Internet Explorer) to **surf** the Web and **e-mail client** software (sometimes contained in the browser) to view, respond to, file, and manage e-mail. Web-based e-mail is available, but you will want Post Office Protocol POP, IMAP, or both in conjunction with Web-based e-mail. Web-based e-mail alone is not sufficient for the real estate professional. Examples of standalone Web-based e-mail are Yahoo Mail and Microsoft's Hotmail.

There are many options for dial-up ISPs. Their charges average about $20 per month with national providers for unlimited access, although lower prices can be found for many local only providers. Cable and DSL access can range from as low as $29.95 per month for a simple single user access point, to hundreds per month for in-home and office-based network **dedicated service.** The advantages (speed) offered by DSL and cable are usually more than enough to offset the additional monthly costs. Satellite can cost $40–$100 per month depending on services and equipment. Wireless connectivity is in the $40 per month range.

Dial-up ISPs are still the most common method of Internet access for most users. The most important consideration for real estate professionals (and anyone, for that matter) in choosing a dial-up ISP is that the ISP has a clean connection through a local phone number or local phone numbers for you to access with no long distance charges. If you travel, you will want a **national ISP** with many dial-up numbers around the country, and also an 800 number for remote areas and when accessing the Internet from a pay phone. This will ensure you can locate and set up a new local access number at an out-of-town location. An important skill for the new real estate professional is to be able to use the Microsoft Windows **dial-up networking wizard.**

The best way to find a good ISP is by word of mouth. Who in your area has the same connectivity requirements as you and is happy with their ISP?

There are many ways to locate good local ISPs. One way is to simply go to *http://TheList.RealTown.com* where you can browse ISPs via area code, state, and more. Also ask friends and business associates which company they use and if they are satisfied with the service they are receiving.

Remember, your ISP is the path through which you conduct your real estate business via the Internet. When shopping for an ISP, consider the following:

- Reliability. Make certain your dial-up ISP has ample connections available so you don't receive any busy signals. Make sure that your ISP has a solid "uptime" record.
- Responsiveness. Are support numbers easily found on their site? If you encounter a problem, can you speak with a human being who will walk you through solutions to your issues?
- Space. How much space will they provide for your e-mail POP3 or IMAP accounts?
- Spam (electronic junk mail). Top-tier ISPs have filters in place to block spam before it reaches your account. Ask potential ISPs if they've configured their e-mail servers to do this and how they determine what is and is not spam.
- Connectivity. Does the ISP provide **cable modem** access, DSL, **56K?** What is the average scheduled monthly downtime; how much time might be lost due to scheduled and emergency system maintenance? What is the average lost time per month during peak and off-peak hours? It's your business, so connect to the Internet effectively.

■ TYPES OF CONNECTIVITY

POTS (PLAIN OLD TELEPHONE SERVICE)

Typical POTS or dial-up connections today are at 24K to 50K and are priced in the $20 per month range for unlimited access. Some ISPs offer, for an additional charge ($6 to $8 per hour), a toll-free dial-up number that is handy when on the road, at airports, pay phones, and other locations requiring toll access.

Consider the following when choosing and periodically evaluating the services of a dial-up ISP:

- How many local dial-up numbers are available?
- Are access numbers available nationally (in the event you are out of town and want to access the Internet)?
- Are toll-free dial-up numbers available (in case you are at an airport or at a location where you have to access the Internet with your **laptop** computer at a pay phone)?
- What is the cost of the toll-free number? ($6 to $8 per hour)

- What is the pricing for unlimited monthly service? (usually less than $21)
- How many e-mail accounts are allowed per subscription?
- Is there an attachment size restriction?
- Is there a limit to the number of e-mail addressees per message?
- What is the storage capacity of your e-mail account?
- Are you notified when your limit is exceeded?
- Are senders notified when your account limit has been exceeded?
- Is there a charge for using your own domain name?
- Are they filtering for spam and blocking e-mail?
- Is there a 24-hour/7 days a week toll-free help line?
- Is there Web access over a browser in case you need to use a different computer?

■ **TIP**
Know the limitations of your ISP.

CABLE

Cable service is provided through cable communication companies in most metropolitan and suburban areas. Cable service is considered high-speed access to the Internet, fitting into the connectivity category referred to as broadband.

Cable modems are great for fast connectivity—up to 100 times faster than ordinary dial-up ISP. In reality, because your speed is determined and restricted by the number of users on your network **node** at any given time, you will probably see speeds range from **500 kbps** to **2 mbps.** That is still many times faster than the typical 56 kbps of the faster modems and dial-up. What this means to you is that a file that takes hours to download on a dial-up connection takes minutes on a cable connection.

Cable modems are not available in all areas. To find out if cable modems are available in your area, call your local cable company. If available, the cost should run about $40 to $50 per month, about twice the cost of dial-up access. However, you are continuously connected to the Internet and your telephone line will be available for phone calls. A shortcoming with cable for the mobile professional is that you can't take the cable with you when you travel. It is not portable so you will still need alternative access to the Internet when you are not at home.

DSL

DSL stands for Digital Subscriber Line and it is faster than normal dial-up. DSL technology uses existing two-wire copper telephone wiring to deliver high-speed data services to businesses and homes. Most ISPs offer **symmetric DSL** data services at seven different speeds. DSL can allow voice and high-speed data to be sent simultaneously over the same line. Because the service is always available, end-users don't need to dial in or wait for call setup. DSL is considered broadband or high speed, an **always on broadband connection** to the Internet, as is cable.

DSL offers greater speeds than dial-up and the added expense is usually worth it for the increased speed. Note that your speed will be restricted by the physical distance your system is from the actual switching facility—called the **central office (CO).** The farther away you are from the CO, the slower your speeds.

SATELLITE

Satellite service provides high-speed connection to the Internet. If you live too far from a phone company office for DSL and there is no cable in your area, satellite Internet access may be worth considering. satellite Internet access does not use telephone lines or cable systems; it uses a satellite dish for two-way (**upload** and download) data communications. Upload speed can be about one-tenth of the 500 kbps download speed. Cable and DSL have higher download speeds, but satellite systems are about ten times faster than a normal **modem.**

A major provider of satellite Internet access is DirecPC. If you are in a very rural area you may not have access to cable or DSL service. With Web sites, software, and file downloads increasing in size, dial-up access may not be a viable answer to a connection problem. The positive side to satellite is that speeds match or exceed those of cable or DSL. The negative side to satellite is equipment cost (up to $500) and per month costs of $40 to $100 (depending on if you want to lease the equipment).

CORPORATE NETWORK (T1/T3)

The corporate network consists of two levels, T1 and T3. T1 is a term coined by AT&T for a system that transfers digital signals at 1.544 megabits per second (as opposed to **ISDN's** mere 64 kilobits per second). T3 is the premium way to access the Internet at up to 30 times (not 3 times) the speed of a T1 line—44.736 megabits of digital data per second.

T1 lines are a popular leased-line option for businesses connecting to the Internet and for ISPs connecting to the Internet backbone. The Internet backbone itself consists of faster T3 connections.

High-speed connections typically are used by businesses for multiple simultaneous users and where high speed is mission critical. T1 and T3 connections are very expensive for the single user and often too costly for the small office to justify. Usually in the $1,000 plus per month range, these connections are generally used by Web hosting companies and larger corporations with many concurrent users.

A fractional T1 line is one or more channels of a T1 service. A complete T1 carrier contains 24 channels, each of which provides 64 kbps. Most phone companies, however, also sell fractional T1 lines, which provide less bandwidth but are also less expensive. Typically, fractional T1 lines are sold in increments of 56 kbps (the extra 8 kbps per channel is used for data management).

FIGURE 4.1 ■ Transfer Size: 4.76 Mb 4,996,190 Bytes Measured In Seconds

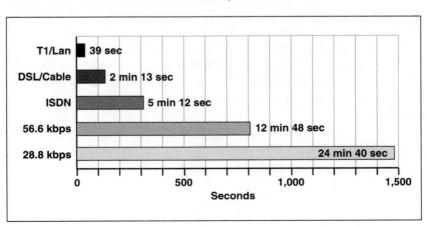

■ BENEFITS OF HIGH SPEED CONNECTIONS

Broadband (high-speed access) will be important to the real estate professional as more MLSs go to Web-based systems. More information will need to be accessed and processed. Faster speed means faster service for the buying consumer.

Broadband is also advantageous when viewing multimedia-based Web information, such as virtual tours and **streaming video** that are now becoming used by more agents when advertising their listings online.

■ CABLE, DSL, AND SATELLITE ACCESS IN YOUR AREA

Information about cable access, DSL, satellite, and other forms of broadband access is important to the new real estate professional for the following reasons:

- Your experience with browser and Web-based MLS systems will be more effective, enjoyable, and productive.
- More of your buyers will begin to require this information, as cable is currently part of the 21st century information infrastructure.
- You can distinguish yourself from the competitors by remaining up to date with broadband access issues in your locality. *It's the little things that make a difference.*

■ WIRELESS ACCESS

The most common form of wireless communication in the real estate industry is the cellular phone. With the right type of hardware and service provider, your computer (or handheld device) can reach the Internet for Web access and e-mail on a wireless connection. Currently there are many aspects of "Wi-Fi" which go beyond the scope of this book. Real estate professionals should consider wireless solutions in their local area as cost and availability permit. Wireless applications include e-mail, Web access, and listing information.

For a glossary of terms see:
http://WirelessGlossary.RealTown.com

■ FREE INTERNET SERVICES

A number of services today offer free access. But be careful with the word *free*. The expression "You get what you pay for" is especially true on the Internet. You may have limited service or you may have to accept advertising. Many of the companies offering free Internet services are going out of business or they are beginning to charge for some of their services. In addition, every e-mail you send might have the "Free Service" advertising attached, which often is not considered professional by your clients and customers. If you are using a free Internet service, send yourself an e-mail message so you can check how the promotion message appears to your recipients. Consider the negative effect of sending an e-mail to a client that may contain the advertising of your competitor.

In the early days of the Web, companies tried to win the race for users by offering services and products for below their cost or free. Of course, this is not a sustainable business model, so it is clear that free services will probably not be long-term offerings. You will find yourself needing to switch to a more permanent access provider before long. Remember, every change of provider causes time delays and marketing problems, so think long and hard before going with a free provider. When choosing any vendor, be sure to take into consideration their capabilities as well as your individual business needs.

There are also free Internet-based e-mail services such as Microsoft's Hotmail and YahooMail. They have their place and purpose, but not as your primary business communication vehicle. Yahoo is a licensed real estate broker,

> **■ TIP**
> Don't use a free, Web-based e-mail as your primary business e-mail solution.

your competition. Would you promote your competition on your business cards and marketing materials? That is what you are doing when you use a Yahoo e-mail address.

■ AMERICA ONLINE (AOL)

AOL is popular, easy to use, gives you multiple screen names, and your kids love it.

AOL's benefits include the following:

- many local dial-up numbers
- an 800 number

- instant messaging (which can be used without being an AOL sub-scriber)
- chat rooms and **communities**

AOL is not, however, a practical stand alone business solution for real estate professionals. Its limitations can include the following:

- e-mail size restriction
- difficulty with attachments—the recipient may be unable to open or view them
- inability to use one's domain in one's return e-mail address
- nonstandard e-mail format
- the fact that AOL does not deliver all of one's e-mail and, in an attempt to filter spam, also filters e-mail one may have been expecting to receive
- its users may be perceived as lacking technical expertise by experienced Internet business users

E-mail messages exceeding a certain size are converted into attachments or bounced back to you—the sender. Many AOL users are annoyed when they have to take an extra step to read their e-mail (that extra step being to "download" an AOL-created attachment) or not be able to read it at all. Even worse, some e-mail messages are not delivered and not bounced, entering e-mail Never Never Land. If you are sending important documents to a customer or client who uses AOL, be sure to confirm that the documents were received and were readable.

More problematic is that once you sign up for AOL, you are locked into an e-mail address that contains the AOL domain (*AOL.com*) and not your own domain. You lose the ability to change your return address in your e-mail client software. When you create a new e-mail message or respond to an e-mail message on AOL, the AOL mail manager will always include your AOL screen name as your return address. Real estate professionals should try to brand their e-mail address (containing their personal domain name) and not an AOL e-mail address. For example, suppose you want your clients to know they can reach you at You@YourDomain.com, a return address not available for use on AOL. How professional would it be for the CEO of IBM to have the following e-mail address: LouGerstner783@aol.com?

America Online is an "edutainment" provider (a mix of education and entertainment). If you enjoy it, then by all means, include AOL in your entertainment budget and increase your technology budget to include another ISP.

AOL AND MLS

It is also important for the real estate professional to know that the AOL browser may not be compatible with certain Internet-based multiple listing service (MLS) systems. As more MLSs become browser-based (and accessible on the Web), real estate professionals will find themselves at a competitive disadvantage if they are depending solely on AOL. In order to access a Web-based MLS, the AOL user may want to minimize AOL and then access the MLS with a full and separate version of Microsoft's Internet Explorer or other browser as recommended by the MLS vendor.

Keep in mind that many of your customers and clients may use AOL. Knowledge of how AOL works and which of your clients and customers use AOL is useful information for you. Because a certain code is required for embedded links to be "hot" links in older versions of AOL, you may want to include that code when e-mailing to AOL users.

AOL FOR CONNECTIVITY

An advantage of AOL is the great number of local dial numbers. One way to use AOL is to use a local dial-up number, minimize AOL, and open your e-mail software such as Microsoft's Outlook or Outlook Express, programmed to retrieve your e-mail sent to a mail account other than AOL.

 TIP
Find an ISP other than AOL for your e-mail services.

Chapter Links:
http://TheList.RealTown.com
http://WirelessGlossary.RealTown.com

■ REVIEW QUESTIONS

1. What's an ISP?

   Answer: ISP stands for Internet Service Provider. An ISP is a company that provides individuals and businesses with access to the Internet, many by purchasing access from larger carriers and then reselling it.

2. What are some examples of broadband connections?

   Answer: Cable, DSL, T1, and T3.

3. What are some of the drawbacks of using AOL as your business e-mail solution?

   Answer:

   E-mail size limitations.

   Difficulty with attachments—the recipient may be unable to open or view them.

   You can't use your domain in your return e-mail address.

   Nonstandard e-mail format.

   AOL does not deliver all your e-mail. In an attempt to filter spam, AOL also filters e-mail you may have been expecting to receive.

   AOL users may be perceived (by experienced Internet business users) as lacking technical expertise.

Chapter Five

Electronic Mail (E-Mail)
A New Way To Communicate

You must break out of your current comfort zone and become comfortable with the unfamiliar and the unknown.
DENIS WAITLEY
http://Motivation.RealTown.com

E-mail is shorthand for electronic mail. E-mail is the term first used to describe the initial message-based communications established by the four universities and the Department of Defense users participating in the original ARPANET, the predecessor to the modern-day Internet. At the time, the messaging system was thought to be an ancillary tool, one that might be useful for speeding up file-passing procedures. It has turned out to be a widely used and popular method of communication—quick, convenient, and nonintrusive. While the telephone can be the "great interrupter"—screaming at you with every ring to "Do me now, do me now, do me now!!!"—e-mail can be answered on one's own schedule, allowing one to take the opportunity to think and compose. This in turn leads to more productive use of one's time overall.

An e-mail message is created by one user (the sender) and sent to one or more other users (recipients), usually through the use of e-mail Client side software, an ISP, and the Internet. There are many different types of e-mail software (e-mail client programs) from which to choose to manage e-mail. This software is sometimes referred to as e-mail management software. Microsoft's Outlook Express is great for the novice and comes bundled with **Microsoft Internet Explorer.** This is free software conveniently available on the Internet. For those who want to combine e-mail software with personal productivity software, the commercial version of Outlook is very powerful. Outlook and Outlook Express are used as examples in this book.

E-mail is more important for your day to day business than a Web site. **Web sites are billboards in the middle of nowhere, yet most people visit their e-mail inbox multiple times a day.** To get the most out of the Internet, you must become a proficient user of e-mail. The secret of success in real estate marketing is to put your name in front of people over and over again. That is why real estate professionals give out pads, calendars, magnets, pens, flyswatters, etc., to keep their name in front of prospective clients. E-mail is another opportunity to put your name in front of your prospective clients.

E-mail has become one of the fastest growing and most widely accepted means of communication since the invention of the telephone. Many people today prefer e-mail communication to the telephone. Some people who may never return a voice mail message will return e-mail promptly.

Although e-mail has been around for many years, it has been available to the general public for only a decade. In a few short years, e-mail has become widespread and generally accepted. In fact, e-mail usage has had a tremendous impact on the way we communicate in total. It makes sense, therefore, that you become an e-mail powerhouse as quickly and effectively as possible.

■ E-MAIL AS A COMMUNICATION TOOL

Because e-mail has been around for the last ten years or so, many real estate professionals believe that they know all there is to know about e-mail. In reality, everyone has much to learn about e-mail communication and e-mail management.

E-mail is software and most people never truly master any software. Your ability to get the most out of software has a lot to do with your vision of what the software can and/or should do for you. Consider word processing software, an application with which many are familiar. In the early days of word processing software, many users' vision of word processing software was simply "no more Wite-Out." It was like a dream come true, a piece of software that allowed you to correct your mistakes *before* you printed them, eliminating the need for correction fluid and correction tape. This was motivation enough to learn how to use the software.

A word processing software vision of "no more Wite-Out" limited many of its early users to taking only minimal advantage of what word processing software had to offer. A word processing software vision of **desktop publishing** greatly expands the possibilities and thinking of the user.

The same is true with e-mail. Many who have been using e-mail for years have an e-mail vision of "send and receive." If that vision is expanded to risk reduction, enhanced client communication, and optimum Internet advertising and marketing, the users' productivity and benefit derived from the software will increase significantly.

> **■ TIP**
> Send yourself an e-mail. Is your permanent e-mail address reflected in the header of the message? If you are using a Web-based system such as AOL, Yahoo, or Hotmail, it will not be. If you are using a free e-mail service, does the advertising in the e-mail advertise another business to the recipients of your e-mail? Could that business be a competitor?

USING E-MAIL EFFECTIVELY IS A SKILL REQUIRING PRACTICE

Learning how to use e-mail software, like learning how to use any software, requires practice. The more you use any particular piece of software, the more things you will learn the software can do—unless, of course, you read manuals, and most people do not. Most people learn to use different **functionality** in software through trial and error—practice.

Practice makes perfect. In the case of developing your skills with e-mail software, you do not need to be perfect, but proficient, and in the case of software, practice makes proficient. To get better at using a **mouse,** for example, play the card game Solitaire as a way of practicing—it is a good way to master mousing techniques. Participating on real estate **Listservs** will give you the opportunity to practice your e-mail skills.

Few real estate professionals can imagine what it would be like to do business without a telephone (or fax or cellular phone, for that matter). The telephone has been the primary means of business communication for years. It

> **■ TIP**
> Sign up for the free RealTalk Listserv at http://RealTalk.RealTown.com

is the old **paradigm** of business communication. The new paradigm of business communication is e-mail. Unless you become an e-mail power user, you will continue to lose a bigger and bigger share of the home buying and selling market.

THE ART OF E-MAIL

Using certain defined protocols will also help you more effectively communicate with e-mail. E-mail users differ in their ability to read and handle e-mail; and senders need to be aware of the skill level and technical limitations of their audience and their audience's **ISP.**

For More Effective E-Mail Communication. The following are several suggestions to improve the effectiveness of your e-mail communications.

- Create useful subject lines—This will help in sorting and locating messages in the future. Some people decide not to open an e-mail based solely on the wording in the subject line. Important messages can contain URGENT in the subject line to attract the recipient's attention (or set to a high priority in your e-mail software). This may be less valuable today with the number of spammers using the Internet, but still a valuable functionality when used in a corporate environment.
- Be as sure as you can be that there are no misspellings. Use the spell check capability of your e-mail software—e-mail is your presence to the world! Protect and project your best image at all times. Have the spell check review each piece of e-mail before you send it.
- Respond promptly—Online users expect it. Check your e-mail multiple times daily, as often as you would your voice mail if not more so. Remember: The first reply usually wins the contact with the prospect. Imagine that you are one of several professionals receiving requests for information from a single prospect.
- AVOID USING ALL UPPERCASE LETTERS. THAT IS LIKE SHOUTING AND IS HARD TO READ.
- Use **emoticons (smileys),** but don't use them excessively—Emoticons are representations of facial expressions made by a series of keystrokes, often producing an image of a face (and expression) sideways. E-mail is not the same as talking on the phone and statements can be misunderstood very easily so sometimes a picture is helpful.

Examples:

:-) Smile

;-) Wink

:-(Frown

- Watch the size of attached files—In the near future many documents and files essential to a real estate transaction will be routinely attached to e-mail, often as pdf files.
- Use good professional judgment when talking about others in an e-mail message. E-mail is easily forwarded.
- Limit your line length to 75 characters—Otherwise, some e-mail programs will not properly wrap the lines. If you use more than 75 characters, the recipient might see "=" (the equals character) at the end of each line and "= 20" (for hard returns).

> ■ **TIP**
> Visit http://eMail.Real Town.com and click on "Emoticons." There you will see more than 100 emoticons to describe your feelings online. Although it is important not to overuse emoticons, their discriminate use can greatly improve the communicative quality of your e-mail.

E-MAIL IS A "FLAT MEDIUM"

Composing e-mail that effectively communicates your message requires a different skill set than traditional business correspondence. Effective e-mail is not purely a function of how well you write. The more you read and write e-mail, the more conscious you will become of the nuances of this new communication medium, and the better you will become at writing e-mail. Writing is a skill that can always be sharpened. As mentioned earlier, practice makes proficiency. A way to practice and improve your writing skills is to contribute to the various real estate-oriented Listserv communities that are available. Carefully read e-mails you get, dissect them, and determine if you would have written them differently.

Because of the convenience, speed, and minimal cost of e-mail, e-mail communications tend to be frequent. There is no gesture, no tone, and no volume. There is no facial expression to help you determine intent, intensity, or emotion. E-mail is just words and from these words, the recipient of e-mail has the task of interpreting the communication.

It is almost too easy to send e-mail. For this reason it is often best not to send an e-mail response when the e-mail you received has affected you emotionally. Once you hit the send button and your e-mail goes charging across the Internet, you usually can't bring it back.

Sometimes, in the heat of the moment, you might be tempted to say something you would otherwise never say. Heed these cautions:

- E-mail lives forever. What you say today might come back to haunt you a year or two down the road.
- E-mail travels at the speed of light. It knows no boundaries and does not require any special ticket to read it. Bottom line: Whatever you send out on the Internet will be there for all to see. There are no secrets in the world of e-mail, so be careful how you handle sensitive information.
- Sarcasm is particularly dangerous to attempt to convey in e-mail.

KNOW YOUR AUDIENCE

Knowing your audience (the people with whom you are attempting to communicate) will enhance the effectiveness of your e-mail communication. The recipient's experience is driven by many factors, some having to do with e-mail consumption habits. For instance, consider these two different scenarios:

Scenario One. Your recipient's e-mail software is running at work throughout the day. The recipient may be conditioned to check incoming e-mail when the background alert sounds (signifying incoming e-mail) or intermittently throughout the day.

Scenario Two. Your recipient is an individual who goes online infrequently.

The more you know about how your client uses e-mail, the more effective your overall communication will be with that client. This will result in a higher level of customer satisfaction.

If your client is an e-mail power user who checks e-mail more than voice mail, your client will expect to receive late-breaking news from you via e-mail right away. As your client may receive more than 100 e-mails per day, it is imperative that you use a succinct, attention-grabbing title in the subject line, such as: "Tuesday 4 P.M.: Oak Trail house on the market again." Make sure you talk to your clients about their e-mail management methods at the beginning of your business relationship, preferably at the time you ask them for their e-mail address.

MORE E-MAIL TIPS

Here are some additional suggestions to help you maximize the efficiency of your e-mail use:

- Use the prefix **mailto:** when entering your e-mail address into a plain text e-mail if you want the recipient to be able to click on the e-mail address and have it open a pre-addressed e-mail response form (e-mail **hotlink**). Some of the more recent versions of e-mail software will work with or without the mailto: prefix but it may be best to assume your target audience has older software. Be careful not to leave blank spaces between the characters.

  Incorrect: MailTo: *You@YourBrand.com*
  Correct: MailTo:*You@YourBrand.com*

- Acronyms can be helpful, but you should not overdo them. These include: BTW = by the way; FYI = for your information; IMHO = in my humble opinion, TTYS = talk to you soon. *http:// Acronyms.RealTown.com.*

- Do not send unsolicited attachments. They tie up the recipient's e-mail while they are being downloaded. Do not send large files without first getting permission from the intended recipient. Many people are cautious about opening attachments because of the epidemic of computer viruses being spread via e-mail attachments.

- Do include portions of the original message in your reply but do not over-quote a prior message in your response—just add enough of the message to put your response in context. This is especially important when posting to a Listserv discussion forum in digest format.

- Use the http:// prefix when you list a Web site's URL in an e-mail. This increases the chances that your recipient will be able to click on the full URL and be transported to the Web page itself. Use of the "www" prefix without the http:// will work with updated e-mail software, but the http:// works with both the older and newer versions. Double-check the URL to make sure the link is working. Putting "InternetCrusade" in a message is far less effective than putting a clickable *"http:// InternetCrusade.com."* You want to make it as easy as possible for customers to work with you online—providing them with a clickable link is much

FIGURE 5.1 ■ Changing to Plain Text

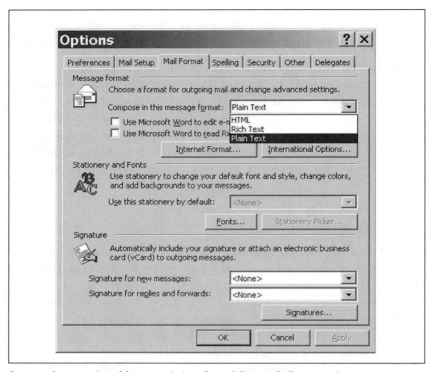

Screen shot reprinted by permission from Microsoft Corporation.

preferred over making them copy and paste a Web address into their browser.

- Send using **plain text** or **rich text format (RTF).** Most e-mail programs can read plain text and RTF. Once you start to add unique formatting—such as html, special characters (bullets, ampersands), different fonts, and color—you run the risk that the recipient will not be able to see your message. When

■ **TIP**
To change to plain text in Outlook go to:
Tools/Options/Mail Format which brings you to the above screen where you select the message format.

in doubt, send in plain text **(ASCII text).** Again, knowing the technology level of your audience is helpful here. It is particularly important to set your e-mail software to plain text when participating in Listserv communities that have **digest versions** (such as **RealTalk**).

Honing e-mail skills requires reviving the lost art of written communication. E-mail offers great advantages over the telephone when properly used. E-mail can be answered at your convenience, letting you think about and craft your replies. E-mail also gives you a written trail of correspondence that can later be recalled in the event of arbitration or litigation.

E-MAIL AS THE ULTIMATE BUSINESS COMMUNICATION TOOL

The Internet continues to infiltrate the lives of real estate professionals and the people they deal with every day: buyers and sellers of real property.

Everywhere we turn we hear about the e-transaction. Clearly, the bulk of communications, document passing, applications, and authorizations required of every real estate transaction will at some point be transported through a combination of e-mail and file-sharing software. Unless you are proficient in e-mail, the e-transaction will pass you by, as will a great opportunity to document your transactions and reduce your business risk.

E-mail is a nonintrusive form of communication, which is why many people would much rather give you an e-mail address than a telephone number. The recipient is not forced to read and respond to e-mail until ready. E-mail allows for deliberate thought if the communication with the sender warrants deliberate thought before a reply is made. It also allows for positive communication without the ritual of telephone tag.

A key to successful Internet marketing of property is rapid response to e-mail inquiries.

Real estate professionals must regard every incoming e-mail message, sent as a result of their Internet advertising and marketing, as they would a ringing telephone. Check your e-mail messages as frequently as you check your voice mail, if not more.

As you continue to provide information to Internet leads who respond to your Internet advertising, you will have the opportunity to build relationships. If the prospect is not in the market to buy immediately, you can continue to provide the prospect with information about available property and the area on a periodic basis, until the prospect is ready to buy. This is an important point. Often Internet buyers may not be ready to purchase for a year or two. E-mail provides you with the capability to send out periodic market updates until the prospect is ready to purchase.

> ### ■ TIP
> Many MLSs today offer an e-mail listing notice functionality that sends an e-mail to the person who subscribed to the service whenever a listing that meets the subscriber's search criteria is entered into the MLS data base. The value to the real estate professional is that the licensee's name will be included in that e-mail notification at the time the listing information is provided to the contact. The secret to success in marketing oneself in the real estate business is putting one's name in front of people over and over again. You cannot do this too much.

■ HOW E-MAIL WORKS (THE DETAILS)

In an Internet-based e-mail system (this can include both the public Internet as well as any variety of closed and semi-closed versions called **Intranets** and **Extranets**) e-mail is composed of messages sent from one point to another by means of a technology known as routing.

Each e-mail message is broken up into tiny fragments—called **packets**—prior to being transmitted from the sender to the recipient(s). These packets contain a **header** (the sender information, recipient information, message identification, and specific position of the packet within the message). This header is used to reassemble the message into a single document once it reaches its final destination(s).

Wrapped between the header and a footer (essentially indicating the end of the packet) is a fragment of the message. Each fragment (packet) is sent electronically to the recipient(s) through the fastest route available at the time of transmission. Each of the fragments of a given message might travel to the destination via a different route. For this reason, the header plays a crucial role in making sure that the message pieces are reassembled correctly on the receiving end.

In proper e-mail addressing the structure for the sender is: SendersName@SendersDomain.com.

This is how every e-mail user is identified in e-mail messaging. Likewise, the recipient is: RecipientsName@RecipientsDomain.com.

SMTP (SIMPLE MAIL TRANSFER PROTOCOL)

The portion of an Internet server that manages the sending of e-mail is normally referred to as **SMTP,** or **Simple Mail Transfer Protocol.** SMTP is told by the sender's e-mail software (the e-mail client) to send the message to the recipient. SMTP then adds the required header and footer and places the message into an **electronic envelope** prior to actually transmitting it over the Internet to the recipient. This envelope contains all of the history for that message: who sent it, how it got to the recipient, time, date, routing, etc. This information can be useful, in turn, when sending a reply to the sender and/or all recipients. If you are having a problem sending e-mail, the problem may relate to your SMTP settings in your e-mail software. It could also be the result of limitations placed upon the **SMTP server** you utilize. Some ISPs require that you use their SMTP server. Others allow you to use the SMTP server of your choice.

For a complex look at SMTP go to:
http://SMTPStory.RealTown.com

Chapter Links:
http://RealTalk.RealTown.com
http://eMail.RealTown.com
http://Acronyms.RealTown.com
http://SMTPStory.RealTown.com

■ REVIEW QUESTIONS

1. Why are e-mail skills so important to today's real estate professional?

   Answer: Many people today prefer e-mail communication to the telephone. Some people who may never return a voice mail message will return e-mail promptly. E-mail is more important for your day-to-day business than a Web site. Web sites are billboards in the middle of nowhere, yet most people visit their e-mail inbox multiple times a day.

2. (T/F) It is easy to write clear and concise e-mail messages.

   Answer: False.

   The more you read and write e-mail, the more conscious you become of the nuances of this new communication medium, and the better you will become at writing e-mail. Writing is a skill that can always be sharpened. Remember, practice makes proficiency. A way to practice and improve your writing skills is to contribute to the various real estate-oriented Listserv communities.

3. List three suggestions that will improve e-mail communication.

   Answer:

   Use descriptive subject lines.

   Be as sure as you can be that there are no misspellings.

   Respond promptly.

Chapter Six

Effective Use of E-Mail— Client Side

Practice doesn't make perfect; practice makes permanent!
DENIS WAITLEY
http://Motivation.RealTown.com

Every e-mail you send is an opportunity to market yourself and your business. Sending large amounts of e-mail means you will be receiving large amounts of e-mail, but you are in control and can hit the delete key and move on. Being an e-mail powerhouse means never having to say you're sorry for hitting the delete key.

■ BECOMING AN E-MAIL POWERHOUSE

An e-mail powerhouse knows how to manage increasing e-mail correspondence for purposes of risk reduction, enhanced **client** communication, and optimum Internet advertising/marketing. An e-mail powerhouse combines the functionality of client side and server side e-mail applications (software) to maximize efficiency and ultimately to increase sales and decrease risk.

Client side refers to applications and software that reside on your computing device (desktop computer, laptop computer, PDA/handheld). Examples of client side applications are Outlook Express, Outlook, and Eudora. These are sometimes referred to as e-mail managers or e-mail clients.

As with all technology, you must first learn what is possible on both the client and server side and then you can select the functionality and services you want to integrate into your business and your business practices.

SETTING UP YOUR CLIENT SIDE E-MAIL SOFTWARE

Most software can be customized for the user. E-mail software is no exception. The functionality that you use most often should be right in front of you where it is easy to reach without searching. The look or view should be the view that lets you work most effectively with the software. Many users never realize the full power of software because they typically use it the way it is set up by the manufacturer. These are called **default** settings.

It is also important to note that much of the functionality in software that you will learn and use is consistent in all Microsoft **Windows** software. You are well on your way to getting the most out of your e-mail software if you are proficient in Windows. Try to take a class on Windows or make use of the online Help feature in your Windows software.

CUSTOMIZING YOUR E-MAIL SOFTWARE

Preview Pane. The preview pane allows you to view the content of an e-mail message without actually opening the message. This can be a great time saver if you receive large volumes of e-mail. To use the preview pane format in the latest version of Outlook Express, go to the "View" button on the tool bar (at the top of your screen) and select "Layout" from the menu. From here you will be able to select (and deselect) the preview pane format. In Outlook, go to "View" and then select "Preview Pane."

Using the preview pane may make you vulnerable to certain types of e-mail viruses. Nevertheless, use the preview pane; make certain to have the latest in antivirus software with the latest virus definitions and the running of frequent virus scans. That is the best protection. Don't let the fear of viruses paralyze you.

Preview Pane Header. While in the preview pane format (again without opening the e-mail), you can see additional information—the identity of the sender of the e-mail; the address(es) the message was sent to;

FIGURE 6.1 ■ Microsoft Outlook Preview Pane

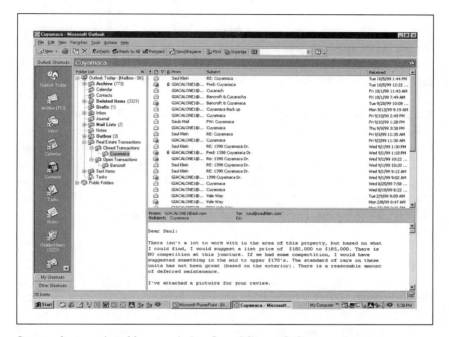

Screen shot reprinted by permission from Microsoft Corporation.

whether copies were sent; to whom the copies were sent; the date the message was sent; and, if there are attachments, the type of file that is attached. You can set up the preview pane header by going to the "View" button, selecting "Layout," and checking "Preview Pane Header."

Message Tool Bars. The two tool bars available to you when creating an e-mail message are standard buttons and formatting bar. Both are set as the default in Outlook Express. To add tool bars, go to "View/Tool-bars." You can also customize your tool bars for your ease of use.

Text Size of E-Mail You Receive. To select font sizes, from "Smallest" to "Largest," simply open Outlook Express, go to the "View" Button, select "Text Size," and choose the appropriate size text for you.

Spell Check. Your e-mail says a lot about you. It is your presence on the Internet. Often people see and read your e-mail long before they meet you in person. To make sure that you don't leave a negative impression because of poor spelling, use the spell check provided by the e-mail software. Set your software so that it checks spelling automatically before you send each piece of e-mail. While it is not perfect (it cannot distinguish between "there and their," both spelled properly and used differently), it will help you put your best foot forward on the Internet.

Return E-Mail Address. More and more people will be adding your e-mail address to their e-mail address book. You'll want to make sure that the e-mail address they see in your e-mail is your **permanent e-mail address. Your return address in your e-mail software should indicate your domain and not the domain of your ISP.** This is one of the most important and one of the most overlooked features of e-mail software. To learn how to change the return address in your e-mail software go to *http://eMailTutorials.RealTown.com.*

Automated Signatures. The content of an e-mail signature is critically important to the support of an online identity. Often the signature is the only picture that recipients have of you and your business. Consider every piece of e-mail a marketing piece. From this point forward, make certain to include the following information in each and every e-mail message that you send:

- Your name
- Your designations
- E-mail and Web address
- Phone and fax
- Auto-responders, if any
- City, state, or area location (for referral purposes)
- Any disclosure information required under state licensing law (e.g., license status, name of broker)

If you have to enter all of the above contact information each time you send an e-mail, it will not be long before you begin to think of all the reasons it is not important to consistently practice such a small thing. Remember "It is the little things that make a difference" as you attempt to differentiate yourself from the competition. **In the age of technology, anything you do more than once should be automated.**

Using the **auto-signature** feature in your e-mail software will allow you to automate your signature so it will appear in every message you send. Most e-mail software will allow you to create multiple signatures depending on the different audiences with whom you may be communicating and the messages you are trying to convey.

It is very important to find that special balance between enough information and way too much information in an **e-mail signature.** For all practical purposes, four to five lines will generally be enough. You can probably fit the required information into that space (with several items on the same line). Any more and you might begin to look like a commercial. The information would be so overwhelming that the reader might just overlook it completely.

To create an e-mail signature in Outlook Express and Outlook, first open the "Tools" menu and select the "Options" choice. Click on the "Signatures" tab (in Outlook, click on the "Mail Format" tab and click on "Signature") to display a **pop-up window** where you can create, edit, and select e-mail signatures.

You can have an unlimited number of e-mail signatures used for many different purposes. Only one signature can be the default signature for an e-mail account. You may, however, have several e-mail accounts—each with its own default signature.

Outlook has a feature to create an electronic business card called a **vCard** that contains detailed contact information on the sender. The vCard comes as an attached file that can be imported into the recipient's Contacts folder. You probably would not want to attach a vCard file to every e-mail you send—people who are not expecting it may not want to open a message with an attached file because of a fear of files with a virus. The vCard signature should not be used on messages sent to Listserv digests.

There are some very powerful ways to employ e-mail signatures. Suppose for example, you wish to provide some specific information to prospects who have written to request information on a particular listing. You might want to have some listing-specific information included in an e-mail signature that you can easily insert into a reply! This is where an auto-responder can be a valuable addition.

■ TIP
Use the multiple signature feature to promptly respond to requests for common information by using pre-written responses.

BUILDING YOUR E-MAIL DATABASE

Don't fall for these kinds of ads: "Purchase 1 million e-mail addresses for $79!" That is not how you want to build your e-mail **database**—your e-mail address book.

There is probably a setting in your e-mail software that captures the e-mail address of all e-mail sent to you and inserts these addresses into your address book. You don't want that either.

You want to build your e-mail address book, your database, first from your existing sphere of influence, and then, by asking everyone you meet for their e-mail address. At every opportunity, obtain an e-mail address for your database. The better you are at classifying and segmenting your database, the more effective you will be at e-mail marketing.

MAKING THE MOST OF E-MAIL EMBEDDED LINKS— DRIVING PEOPLE TO YOUR WEB SITE

The first thing most people check when they go online and the place where individuals spend most time online is their **e-mail inbox.** If you want to reach people on the Internet, don't wait for them to come to your Web site, go where the people are—meet them at their inbox.

One way to drive prospects and clients to your Web site or to the published material you have on the Web is to push information at them. You send an e-mail message that contains some information of value or other compelling reason to want to read or see more at your Web site. An **embedded link** is a handy feature that encourages easy access to your Web site.

Clicking on the **link** embedded in an e-mail message will transport the consumer over the Internet to your Web site. By using the embedded link, the potential customer can quickly and conveniently click, and be at your Web site.

Even the Web novice can point and click. He or she does not have to know how to open a browser to type in a URL (possibly typing in the wrong URL or making a typo); all that is required is to point and click.

An embedded link is text in an e-mail message or a document that, when clicked on, either opens a properly addressed blank e-mail message or links out to a Web site on the Internet. This is referred to as a hotlink or a **hyperlink.**

E-Mail Hyperlink. To create an e-mail hyperlink and have it function in any e-mail software, use MailTo: in front of the e-mail address, with no space after MailTo:

Example: *MailTo:Me@YourDomain.com*

The software assumes that you want it to be a hyperlink and will make it one. To remove the hyperlink, hit the backspace after you finish typing the e-mail address.

Web Hyperlink . To create a Web hyperlink in an e-mail message and have it function in any browser, begin typing http:// and your software will create the link to the URL that follows http://.

Note: This technique also works in Word, PowerPoint, etc. Some modern software will create the link by typing the "www" prefix but you will reach more people if you use the http:// prefix.

Just by typing http://, the link becomes "hot" in the e-mail or the document you are working in (Outlook, Word, PowerPoint, etc.). Creating embedded links in this manner is a Windows functionality.

Note: This technique does not work when sending e-mail to recipients using older versions of AOL. If you want to send embedded links to those AOL users, you must embed the link in html code. **HTML** (Hypertext Markup Language—the base code for creating Web pages) is not at all difficult to use for embedding links. Here is the format for AOL users:

```
<a href="http: //InternetCrusade.com">Click Here</a>
```

The AOL user will see "Click Here." When they click on it, they will be taken to the URL *http://InternetCrusade.com.*

If you are sending e-mail to AOL users, be sure to use this technique to make your links "hot." You will notice in the signature of many real estate professionals that they include the AOL linking code in addition to the customary embedded link.

SETTING FONT STYLE AND SIZE

Setting the font style and size is a function of the type of system you are using. For example, plain text is viewable by older e-mail software and is recommended for listserv postings.

On the other hand, rich text format (RTF) is viewable by newer browsers and is the recommended setting to ensure your e-mail can be seen by almost everyone; use plain text for Listservs, however. HTML should be used only when you know that the people you are sending your e-mail to have e-mail software capable of viewing e-mail written in this format. HTML format allows for more color and design than plain text and RTF.

SETTING UP YOUR E-MAIL SOFTWARE TO RETRIEVE E-MAIL FROM YOUR E-MAIL ACCOUNTS AND SEND E-MAIL THROUGH MAIL SERVERS (POP3 AND SMTP)

Your e-mail client software is not preset to check your e-mail at your specific ISP. To make that happen, you first need to set the system to know where to go to check your mailbox for new e-mail (at your POP3 server) and where to go to send e-mail (from your SMTP server). If you are not sure of the particular settings, check with an experienced advisor or friend so you make sure your e-mail is working properly.

CREATING FOLDERS

Top-tier e-mail software (such as Microsoft Outlook and Eudora) offers rich tools for managing and separating incoming messages into **folders** that can be customized to fit your way of managing information.

It might surprise you to learn that many top professionals easily receive more than 100 messages per day. These can range from the personal message, to the transaction-specific, to the prospective inquiry, to the information-sharing Listserv messages. One hundred per day, 3,000 per month, 36,000 per year! **Without effective e-mail management skills, you will be in e-mail overload.**

Effective e-mail management is an absolute requirement if you intend to become an e-mail powerhouse and to make the most of the Internet. Create folders that reflect your business and your method of communication filing. Often for real estate professionals this involves creating a folder for every listing or for every client, buyer, or seller. You then sort the e-mail received into each folder. Creating a folder can be as easy as four clicks:

- Right Click
- New Folder

FIGURE 6.2 ■ Microsoft Outlook Folder Listings

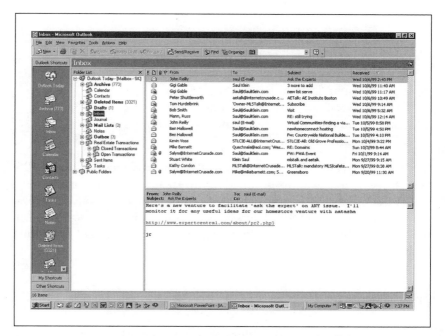

Screen shot reprinted by permission from Microsoft Corporation.

- Name Folder
- OK

To manage e-mail effectively you must work to keep your inbox below 20 e-mail messages. Having more than 20 e-mail messages in your inbox may require scrolling to find e-mail in your inbox. Scrolling through e-mail you have already read is like handling the same piece of paper more than once, which any time-management program will tell you is a waste of time.

One method is to sort manually as soon as the message arrives by **dragging and dropping** it into the appropriate folder. This keeps all communications about that property transaction or client in a specific location—easy to find (or search for) on demand.

Folder examples:

Listings
Active Listings (subfolder under "Listing")
123 Main Street (sub-subfolder under "Active")
322 Apple Lane (sub-subfolder under "Active")
Inactive (subfolder under "Listing")
Pending (subfolder under "Listing")
100 Elm Street (sub-subfolder under "Pending")
Closed (subfolder under "Listing")

You can create rules to automatically move any message about 123 Main Street into the appropriate folder (instead of your inbox).

In the event that an active listing becomes a pending sale, it is simple to move the entire 123 Main Street folder to its new location as a subfolder of "Pending." Usually this is just a dragging and dropping procedure.

CREATING RULES

It is possible to build folders and have incoming e-mail sorted directly to the designated folder without the e-mail first going to your inbox. The sorting is done in Outlook Express and Outlook by using **rules,** where you select the **conditions** and the **actions** for the filtering. Using rules can save a lot of time and reduce the number of times you handle certain e-mail messages. You'll want to remember to check your folders periodically because you won't be seeing the new messages appear in your Inbox.

Example:

Conditions:
"Where the 'From' Line contains people"
"Where the 'Subject' Line contains specific words"
"Where the message is marked as a Priority"
"Where the message body contains a specific word"

Actions:
"Move it to a specific folder"
"Copy it to a specific folder"
"Delete it"
"Forward it to People"

Specific Example:
Condition(s): All e-mail with 123 Elm Street in the subject or body of an e-mail
Action: Move it to the folder titled 123 Elm Street

For more information on Personal Information Management and Managers go to: http://PIM.Realtown.com

BUILD DISTRIBUTION LISTS OR GROUPS FOR EVERY TRANSACTION

Creating **groups** will allow you to easily communicate by e-mail with all the participants in a transaction by sending a single e-mail addressed to the group. As an example, to notify everyone in the transaction that there will be a walk-through inspection on a specific date, address an e-mail to the specific group or **distribution list** for that transaction and it will be sent to all transaction participants in one action.

Example:
Transaction: 123 Crusade Drive

Transaction Participants:
Buyer
Seller
Lender
Attorney
Escrow company
Title insurance company
Pest control company
Appraiser
Buyer's Broker
Seller's Broker
Filtering Incoming E-mail

Basic E-mail Actions. Reply—Addresses e-mail to the e-mail address(s) in the From field

Reply to All—Addresses e-mail to the e-mail address(s) in the From, To, and Cc fields

Forward—Opens an untitled e-mail message containing the entire message with any attachments (note that a Reply or Reply To All will not include the attached file; the Forward action will)

CREATING A NEW E-MAIL MESSAGE

To create a new e-mail message follow these steps.

1. Determine the addressees to whom you will be sending the e-mail. Make certain that all of the addresses are correctly entered in the desired location (To, Cc, Bcc). Use the **address book** for most addresses, as these will usually be correct. **Double-clicking** on a name places it in the desired location, thus eliminating the need to type the address. **Auto-filling** of e-mail addresses into the address boxes will also save time and errors. If you type the first few letters of the person's name, the latest versions of e-mail software will auto-fill the rest. If two or more names have the same first three characters, the software will give you a list from which to choose the correct addressee.

2. Give the message a descriptive title in the subject line. Often this is the only introductory information the recipient has on which to base a decision to read or delete.

■ TIP
Select your subject line language carefully.

Make sure the subject tells the reader enough to help the reader decide to open the message. Some people set up spam filters that look for key words in the subject line and automatically delete the message. These could include words such as *sex and Viagra,* but could also include a word such as *free.*

3. Type or paste the body of the message. You should select a **universal type of font,** or the recipient's system might replace it. Usually Arial, Times, Times New Roman, Courier, and Serif will be available and are considered to be universal. Business e-mail messages should be concise and to the point. Use short paragraphs. Many users receive hundreds of messages per day. Make sure that yours is read.

4. Add your signature to the message. Most e-mail software allows the signature to be automated; some allow you to choose from multiple signatures. You might elect to have the signature added as a default.

To create a signature, go to:
http://eMailTutorials.RealTown.com

5. Add attachments. Remember that attached files grow in size when broken into packets for e-mailing. Many ISPs have a **file-size restriction.** Some ISP limitations are as small as 1 mb. Make sure that the recipient is willing to receive messages with large attachments BEFORE you send attachments. You want to avoid causing a major inconvenience on the receiving end. There is nothing worse than waiting minutes upon minutes for one file to download over a dial-up connection. Not everyone has cable, DSL, or satellite speed!

6. Click on "Send" when you are ready to let the message go out to the SMTP server for delivery to the addressees. Once you click "Send," you cannot recall your message so check for content and proper addressees. Before clicking "Send," be sure to check that you have properly added the attachment. Note that some people are hesitant to open messages with attachments because of a fear of viruses—you might want to contact recipients ahead of time so they know to look out for your attachment.

ADDRESSING E-MAIL

For better efficiency, the members of your team or work group should understand the fundamentals of addressing e-mail correspondence.

"To." The "To" address field is the one you are directing the communication to, requesting action or a response.

"Cc." The "Cc" address field receives the e-mail for information purposes only and usually is not expected to reply.

"Bcc" (blind carbon copy). The "Bcc" address field receives the e-mail for informational purposes only, unknown to the other recipients. If the Bcc field is not visible, try clicking on "View" and then clicking on "Bcc."

Note: A risk in using "Bcc" is that the Bcc recipient is unknown to the rest of the addressees, if the Bcc recipient hits "reply to all" and sends a message, then the Bcc recipient will become known to the group, which could create an embarrassing situation.

Use Bcc to send an e-mail to a list of people without disclosing their e-mail address to everybody else on the list or to anyone to whom the e-mail would be forwarded. This works much better than disclosing a long list of e-mail addresses in the To or the Cc fields; not only do e-mails with long lists of addressees look unattractive, but all those revealed

TIP
Some ISPs limit the number of addressees allowed in an e-mail message. Find out if your ISP has a limitation and if it does, what that limitation is.

addresses become easy prey for spammers to harvest and sell.

As previously mentioned, creating address groups, or lists of people that you will be sending messages to on a regular basis, is good e-mail management. By grouping individuals, you will no longer have to add or click each person in the address book to include him or her in the e-mail. Sending a message to the group will be the same as sending one copy to each of the group members.

ATTACHING FILES

Many of the files essential to a real estate transaction are routinely attached to e-mail.

When attaching files, it is important to consider the size of the file. With the limited bandwidth available to many using the Internet, a large file may create problems for the recipient. The recipient may also lack the proper software version to open and read an attachment or view a graphic, thus presenting incompatibility issues. If, for example, you send a Word document using a version newer than the recipient has, the recipient won't be able to read it.

More importantly, users receiving large attachments might not have the ability to selectively **download** attachments. Many times, the attachment will start downloading whether the intended recipient wants it or not! Imagine being on the receiving end of a 5 MB attachment at a busy point in your day and

TIP
Know the size of an attachment before you send it and know the capability of the person to whom you are sending.

being forced to complete the download. If you were not expecting the file, you would not be very fond of the sender.

OPENING FILE ATTACHMENTS

In both Outlook Express and Outlook, an **icon** that looks like a paper clip next to an e-mail message heading is an indication that there is at least one file attached to the message. You can find out how many and what types of files are attached by opening (double-clicking) the e-mail message (not the attachment). A new line under the subject line will appear telling you the name, type, and size of the attachment.

ATTACHMENT FILE TYPES

Assuming that you do want to open an attachment, your system will need to know what type of file it is and what application to use to open the file. This is the main purpose of the file extension (usually the three letters following a period in the file name; e.g., in "test.doc", the file is a "doc" file that would be opened by your word processor). Double -click the file name and the system opens it in the **associated application.** If you want to keep the attachment on your hard drive after the e-mail message is deleted, you need to save the file. Right-click the attachment in the e-mail message and select Save or Save As and save to the most appropriate location, usually a location on your desktop or in My Documents.

ASSOCIATED FILE TYPES

Windows comes with a series of default settings that tell Windows which programs to use when opening certain file types. Every time you install a new **application program,** it instructs Windows to use that application program when opening certain file types. Usually, the following file types will open in the related applications:

- Images (**.gif, .jpg, .bmp**)—Web browser or graphics program
- Documents (.doc, .txt)—Word processor
- Video (**.mov, .avi,** .ram, **.qt**)—Media Player, QuickTime, Real-Player, etc.
- Web page (.htm, .html)—Web browser
- Presentation (.ppt)—PowerPoint
- Spreadsheet (.xls, .wbk)—Excel

CHANGING FILE ASSOCIATIONS

You can change file associations manually or add more file types through the File Association features of Windows. To associate a file type, go to the Windows Desktop and double-click the "My Computer" icon. Click the "View" menu and select "Folder Options." Click on "File Types" and locate the type you want from the list.

Click on the file type to change and then click the "Edit" button. Once the dialog box opens, click the "Edit" button in the lower half; a new window opens that says "application used to perform this action." Note the "Browse" button next to it.

Click the "Browse" button and browse to the program file that you will use to open this file type from now on. Double-click it and you will be ready to save the process.

Note: If you are having trouble locating the files to associate, your best bet will be to look first in the "Program Files" folder. This is where applications (.exe, .bat, .vbs) usually will be located. Alternatively, you can click the "Start" button and then "Find" the application.

Chapter Links:
http://eMailTutorials.RealTown.com

■ REVIEW QUESTIONS

1. What is the purpose of the "Preview Pane" in e-mail software?

   Answer: The preview pane allows you to view the content of an e-mail message without actually opening the message. Using the preview pane may make you vulnerable to certain types of e-mail viruses. Nevertheless, use the preview pane; just make certain to have the latest in antivirus software with the latest virus definitions and the running of frequent virus scans. Don't let the fear of viruses paralyze you.

2. The content of an e-mail signature is critically important to the support of an online identity. Often the signature is the only picture that recipients have of you and your business. What items should be included in your e-mail signature?

Answer:

Your name
Your designations
E-mail and Web address
Phone and fax
Auto-responders, if any
City or area location (for referral purposes)
Any disclosure information required under state licensing law
(e.g., license status, name of broker)

3. Why is it important to learn how to create folders in your e-mail
   client software?

   Answer: Effective e-mail management is an absolute requirement if you intend to become an e-mail power-user and to make
   the most of the Internet. Create folders that reflect your business and your method of communication filing. Often for real
   estate professionals this is the creation of a folder for every
   listing or for every client, buyer, or seller. You can then sort the
   e-mail received into each folder.

Chapter Seven

Effective Use of E-Mail— Server Side

Success is almost totally dependent upon drive and persistence. The extra energy required to make another effort or try another approach is the secret of winning.
DENIS WAITLEY
http://Motivation.RealTown.com

The term *server side* refers to services and functionality available through a server (usually through an ISP), which is connected to the Internet and "always on," 24 hours a day, seven days a week, and 365 days a year.

■ THE PERMANENT E-MAIL ADDRESS (PROVIDED BY AN E-MAIL HOST, "SERVER SIDE")

Your e-mail address is your identity on the Internet. We have discussed this in previous chapters. You want an e-mail address that does not change just because you change from one ISP to another or from one real estate company to another. Your ISP move may simply be a move from dial-up service to broadband (cable and DSL). Changing your ISP will force you to change your e-mail address, unless you have your own domain and have used it in conjunction with an e-mail account to create a **permanent e-mail address.**

When you change ISPs, you will receive a new e-mail address (often a **user name** at your new ISP.com) and a password. If you discontinue your previous ISP account, e-mail sent to your old ISP e-mail address (your old ISP user name) will probably not be forwarded to your new

ISP and will bounce back to the sender as undelivered or be an unreceived, and thus an unresponded to, e-mail. This may give the appearance that you are no longer in business—a negative and potentially costly impression. In addition, you must now re-invest in all your marketing materials—business cards, signs, stationery—anything bearing the old e-mail address must now be destroyed and replaced with updated information.

It doesn't make any sense to train **customers** and clients (your **sphere of influence**) to send e-mail to an address that may not exist in the future. As every piece of e-mail is a marketing piece, it makes sense to have your permanent e-mail address in as many pieces of e-mail as possible. You want to train your clients to send e-mail to you at an e-mail address at a domain you own and control. Once you have a permanent e-mail address, you can change the return address in your e-mail software reflecting that e-mail address. This may sound like a little thing, but remember it is the little things that make a difference when you are working to differentiate yourself from your competition. With a permanent e-mail address, all your branding efforts and dollars spent to create an e-mail presence will, over the years, create a cumulative result. Having a permanent e-mail address will prove much more cost-effective than diffusing your marketing dollars over the years on e-mail addresses that no longer exist because you changed ISPs or brokerage firms.

Consider the cost of potential lost business. When you change Internet service providers your old e-mail address is no longer functional. You will not receive any e-mail sent to the old e-mail address. Not receiving all of your e-mail could be costly to you.

If the day after you change from one ISP to another, a past client sends you an e-mail requesting that you call about listing a $3 million home and you do not receive that e-mail, you cannot respond to e-mail you do not receive and you will probably lose that business.

> ■ **TIP**
> Create a permanent e-mail address today. All you need is your own domain and e-mail forwarding.

In addition to the cost of lost business, every time you change e-mail addresses you will need to reprint your business cards and marketing materials. This is a minor cost when compared to the cost of lost business, but a loss nonetheless.

FIGURE 7.1 ■ E-Mail Forwarding Diagram

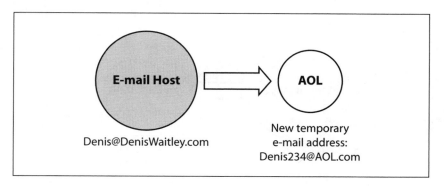

HOW DO I OBTAIN A PERMANENT E-MAIL ADDRESS?

The foundation of your permanent e-mail address is your own domain as opposed to the domain of your ISP. As long as you are in business, you will benefit by owning and using your own domain as the foundation of your online communication and marketing plan.

If the ISP providing you with your connectivity also provides you with a POP account such as POP3 (most do provide a mail account), they may host your domain and point e-mail sent to You@YourDomain to that POP3 account. If this is the case, ask if there is any additional charge for forwarding the e-mail addressed to your domain to the POP3 account. Also find out what other e-mail functionality the ISP provides with your POP3 account. POP3 account functionality brings a whole new level of communication control to the new real estate professional.

An alternative way to accomplish this is to have your domain host (a company other than your ISP) forward mail sent to your domain to the POP3 account at your ISP. If you change ISPs, have your domain host forward mail sent to your permanent e-mail address to your new ISP. E-mail forwarding will set you free!

E-MAIL FORWARDING

Mail sent to your domain is forwarded to the ISP of your choice. Mail sent to Denis@DenisWaitley.com is forwarded to Denis's AOL account.

Denis then changes dial-up companies and signs up at Earthlink where he is given a new e-mail address (User Name), Denis@Earthlink.net. He doesn't give anyone this user name; he simply changes the

FIGURE 7.2 ■ Changing an E-Mail Forwarding Address

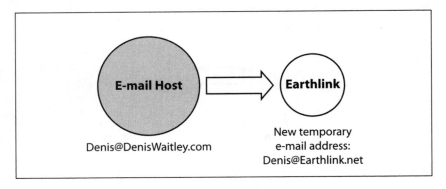

FIGURE 7.3 ■ Changing an E-Mail Forwarding Address

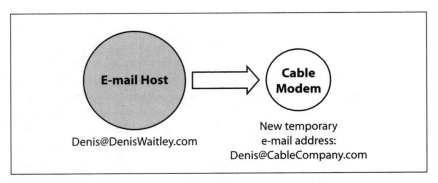

forwarding of e-mail sent to Denis@DenisWaitley.com from AOL to Earthlink.

Mail sent to Denis@DenisWaitley.com is forwarded to Denis's Earthlink account.

Denis then changes from Earthlink to a cable company for a high-speed connection, where he is given a new e-mail address (user name), Denis@Cable Company.com. He doesn't give anyone this user name; he simply changes the forwarding of e-mail sent to Denis@ DenisWaitley.com from Earthlink to the cable company.

■ **TIP**
For more information on obtaining a permanent e-mail address go to: http://PermanentEmail Address.RealTown.com

Denis's e-mail address is portable. He can take it with him when he changes from one ISP to another. Why? Because he owns it—as a real estate agent, you have probably often discussed the benefits of owning versus renting.

UNLIMITED E-MAIL ADDRESSES (PROVIDED BY AN E-MAIL HOST, "SERVER SIDE")

Sometimes called *e-mail forwarding, or star e-mail forwarding, unlimited addressing allows for all e-mail sent to your domain to be sent to your POP3 or mail account.

Examples are:
Anything@You.com
Joe@You.com
CNN@You.com

E-mail addresses can be made up on the fly with no technological intervention because all e-mail sent to your domain will be delivered to the POP3 account mailbox of your choice. This functionality can be used for ad tracking and spam control.

Ad Tracking. By using different e-mail addresses in different advertising, you can track the results of each ad. If, for example, you run an ad in the *Journal*, have all those interested in more information on the property send an e-mail to: JournalProperty1@YourBrand.com.

If you also run an ad in the *Gazette* the same weekend, have all those interested in more information on the property send an e-mail to: GazetteProperty1@YourBrand.com. All e-mail will be sent to the same POP3 account, but now you know the source of the lead and over time will be able to know which publication serves your advertising and budget needs better.

To take e-mail and classified ads one step further, whenever you run a classified ad, the e-mail address you give should be set up with an **auto-responder.** This would allow you to deliver much more detail on the property than you would or could in a classified ad. An auto-responder is an immediate response to an interested party's e-mail (with impressive response time); you now

■ **TIP**
Owning your own domain gives you the ability to take advantage of certain powerful "server side" e-mail functionality.

have captured the e-mail address of the prospect, which will allow you to send an e-mail when you are at your computer.

Spam Control. One of your most valuable technology assets is your own domain. It allows you to maintain a permanent e-mail address. To avoid having spam sent to your permanent e-mail address, make up a temporary e-mail address the next time you are asked for an e-mail address on the Web. Having unlimited e-mail addressing functionality allows you to do this on the fly.

When you are asked for an e-mail address for any purpose other than business or personal use, make one up that pertains to the situation and the particular commerce. When signing up at CNN, for example, give the e-mail address CNN@YourName.com. If you sign up for the *New York Times* online, give the e-mail address NYT@YourName.com. If you purchase a new bicycle and the bike shop wants an e-mail address, give them Bikes@YourName.com. If your e-mail host is providing you with unlimited e-mail address functionality, any e-mail sent to your domain is then forwarded to your e-mail account. If you begin to receive e-mail about buying camping gear or running gear addressed to Bikes@YourName.com, you can assume your e-mail address has been sold or traded by the bicycle company. If the volume of e-mail sent to that made-up address—Bikes@YourName.com-becomes too much of a burden to delete, you can create rules and filters as discussed in a prior chapter, **routing** that e-mail to the folder of your choice, which could be your Deleted Items folder.

> ■ **TIP**
> Use unlimited addressing to better manage your flow of e-mail. Ask your e-mail host for this functionality, which should be provided to you at no extra cost. A step above this concept would be aliasing, in which new e-mail accounts are set up.

Unlimited e-mail addresses also help ensure you receive e-mail that is intended for you. Misspellings of names, as long as the sender gets the domain correct, will still be sent to your e-mail account at your ISP. The unlimited e-mail address feature can also be set up where the address is first entered into your e-mail system, through a convenient, easy-to-use Web interface (something you can do without having to contact your ISP).

■ UNSOLICITED E-MAIL—SPAM DEFINED

Spam is typically (although not always) e-mail that is sent to you by someone who has no prior or existing relationship with you. Spam is also called unsolicited commercial e-mail (UCE); unsolicited bulk e-mail (UBE); or junk e-mail. Often the sender's address is not visible or traceable, with the content of the e-mail merely directing you to a Web site.

Types of spam include:

- pornography and unethical senders such as the Nigerian Scheme;
- chain letters, hoaxes, and urban legends;
- legitimate offers from legitimate senders; and
- business spam from your associates.

The use of the term *spam* to mean unsolicited e-mail comes from a Monty Python skit in which all the participants in a café began to chant the word "spam." This chanting drowned out any other conversation, which, if you think about it, is exactly what e-mail spam does—it drowns out all other e-mail. SPAM is actually a luncheon meat product of Hormel Foods. Hormel lost the case protecting their trademark; now uppercase SPAM is the Hormel product and lowercase spam is unsolicited e-mail.

Unlike direct mail or telemarketing, e-mail marketing has very little cost. As a result, despite extremely low response rates, spammers can make a profit. The more e-mail a spammer sends, the greater the profit potential, with costs remaining fairly constant.

HOW DO SPAMMERS OBTAIN YOUR E-MAIL ADDRESS?

Spammers have software that scans Web pages, newsgroups, and other online documents to harvest e-mail addresses. There are also programs that generate millions of e-mail messages using combinations of letters and numbers in front of a domain name, with the hopes that one will be a legitimate functioning e-mail address, thus delivering the message of the spammer to someone who may have an interest in what is being offered in the spam e-mail. One source of e-mail addresses for spammers is the domain registry directory where e-mail addresses of domain owners are available to the world. Another source is online rosters that were created without an anti-scraping feature.

The key to reducing and managing spam is to filter on both the client side and the server side. Also, keep your primary e-mail address away from the spammers by using aliases and the unlimited e-mail address feature along with filters. Your first line of defense is the delete key. A good product to assist you in spam control is e-MailPlus, offered by InternetCrusade (information available at *http://InternetCrusade.com* under products).

■ WEB-BASED E-MAIL

Web based e-mail is a feature of an e-mail account that gives you the ability to read, reply, delete, and forward your e-mail from any point of Internet access. This includes someone else's computer, a kiosk, Web TV, etc. Internet-accessed e-mail gives you e-mail capabilities without access to your personal computer.

BENEFITS OF WEB BASED E-MAIL

Web-based e-mail offers several major benefits. These benefits include the following:

- You don't have to have your computer with you or be at your computer.
- Web-based e-mail doesn't require any special software.
- You can access your e-mail anywhere there is Internet access—whether at a client's home, an airport, at the house of a friend—anywhere there is an appliance with access to the Internet. From the cellular phone to the Internet **kiosk** at a grocery store, e-mail access is becoming ubiquitous.
- Internet-accessed e-mail can also be used to review and, if necessary, delete large files before you attempt to download them.

There are other types of Internet-accessed and Internet-based e-mail systems providing free services, such as Yahoo and Hotmail. While they may have their place based on the way you use the Internet, for business purposes it makes sense to respond to your business contacts through a Web interface that is part of your e-mail system and branded with your domain. Some free Internet e-mail providers may terminate your account if they discover you are using it for business purposes.

■ AUTO-RESPONDER: 21ST CENTURY VERSION OF FAX ON DEMAND

A ten-page report may be a little too much for faxing or for a classified ad, but e-mail is another story. An auto-responder can send property information to interested parties automatically at the push of a button, at the speed of light. It is a much less expensive way to send relocation material to prospects. In order to receive the report, the prospect must provide his or her e-mail address in an e-mail message sent to the auto-responder requesting the information you are offering. You are giving something of value (information) in return for something of value (the prospect's e-mail address, which is automatically sent to you by the auto-responder). This is an acceptable method of capturing e-mail addresses to add to your database. When someone requests to be removed from your database, do so immediately.

Some e-mail software contains **auto reply** capability. It is limited, however, in that it is only functioning when you are connected to the Internet. It can only reply when you are online. A Web-based auto-responder, on the other hand, is 24/7/365 (always on the Internet, 24 hours a day, 7 days a week, 365 days a year—even when you are not).

> **■ TIP**
> An auto-responder used in conjunction with an automated e-mail signature is an effective method of Internet marketing.

Let's go back to that ten-page report on your listing. You paste the report into the auto-responder and assign it to the e-mail address 123RiverStreet@YourBrand.com. It's as simple as that.

Give the seller a handful of your business cards with 123RiverStreet@YourName.com written on the back and ask the seller to give them out to anyone who is interested in the property. Now the seller is helping you spread the word.

Include the auto-responder e-mail address in your classified advertisements, allowing the distribution of more complete information about the property via e-mail in exchange for an e-mail address of an interested party. You are also building your e-mail database. This type of marketing is quantifiable, inexpensive, and very much a marketing **differentiator**.

Using this great technology tool, you can inexpensively and conveniently deliver any information you want to make available to a consumer who may be interested in your listings, your buyer services, or any other valuable information you wish to make available to the public.

FIGURE 7.4 ■ Auto-Responders: 21st Century Fax on Demand

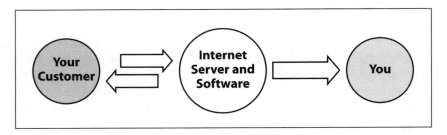

Every ad you run on listings should include an auto-responder offering more detail on the subject property, such as listings@your-name.com or ForSale@YourName.com.

For a sample of the speed of an auto-responder, send a blank message to ARInfo@InternetCrusade.com.

http://AutoResponders.Realtown.com

■ LISTSERV (MAIL LISTS)

Listserv is a term referring to a type of Internet mail account. Its functionality can have different uses, one being a type of online newsletter. Because it is server side, a listserv can avoid certain ISP addressee delivery limitations. Listservs will be discussed in greater detail in the chapter on **online community.** They are great for "haves and wants."

HOW DO LISTSERVS WORK?

The list of a listserv is a database of e-mail addresses of subscribers to the list. E-mail is sent to the list from bona fide members and then simultaneously released to the entire list of subscribers.

POSTING TO THE LIST

There is a specific procedure to follow when posting to a list. First open a blank e-mail message and address it to the e-mail address of the list. Make sure you enter the appropriate subject in the subject line, which describes the content of your message. Type the message and

FIGURE 7.5 ■ Listserv Flow of Information

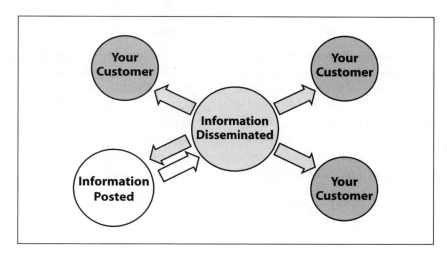

make sure your short **signature** is included. Send the message to the address of the listserv. If you were using a listserv as a newsletter, the address of the listserv could be something like VIP@YourName.com.

Check the subject line to make sure it correctly reflects the topic on which you are commenting. An attention-grabbing subject line will entice people to read your message.

For more information on listservs go to:
http://Listservs.RealTown.com

■ E-MAIL ACTION PLANS

Want to create a publishing plan with different messages going out to different individuals on different days? One way to accomplish this is using server side e-mail action plans, which, once again, because they are server side, will avoid ISP sending limitations.

For more information, go to:
http://eMailActionPlans.RealTown.com

Chapter Links:
http://PermanentEmailAddress.RealTown.com
http://Listservs.RealTown.com
http://eMailActionPlans.RealTown.com

■ REVIEW QUESTIONS

1. Why is it so important to have a permanent e-mail address?

   Answer: Your e-mail address is an asset of your business and you invest in it every day. If you discontinue your previous ISP account, e-mail sent to your old ISP e-mail address (your old ISP user name) will probably not be forwarded to your new ISP and will bounce back to the sender as undelivered or just be an unreceived, and thus an unresponded to, e-mail. This may give the appearance that you are no longer in business—a negative and potentially costly impression.

2. What are some of the uses of unlimited e-mail addresses and e-mail aliases?

   Answer: Because e-mail addresses are unique identifiers, they can be used to: control spam; track advertisements; and generally, source leads.

3. What is a Listserv?

   Answer: Listserv is a term referring to a type of Internet mail account. Its functionality can have different uses, one being a type of online newsletter, another to create a discussion group, and even an online community. Because it is a server side tool, a listserv can avoid certain ISP addressee delivery limitations.

Chapter Eight

Creating an E-Mail Marketing Strategy

Our limitations and success will be based, most often, on our own expectations for ourselves. What the mind dwells upon, the body acts upon.

DENIS WAITLEY
http://Motivation.RealTown.com

One of the primary advantages of selecting and using a top-tier e-mail client software is that you have some powerful tools available for retrieving, storing, and maintaining e-mail addresses in an easy-to-use format. This tool can be a simple e-mail address book or a powerful **contact management system.**

Outlook Express is somewhere in the middle of these two extremes. It offers some sophisticated ability to store and view detailed contact information. Outlook, on the other hand, meets the criteria of the most powerful systems. In Outlook, not only can you store and retrieve detailed information about each contact, you can also link those contacts to activities, appointments, files, messages, and other journal-style information. In this regard, Outlook Express is simply an e-mail manager. Outlook is a full-fledged contact and e-mailing system, which is also known as a PIM (Personal Information Manager) or personal productivity software.

Whatever system you select, make certain you learn and use the address book functions.

■ COLLECTING E-MAIL ADDRESSES

To conduct e-mail marketing campaigns, you will need e-mail addresses.

Ask for e-mail addresses at every opportunity. Just asking for someone's e-mail address says something positive about you to Internet users and will differentiate you from your competition. Another differentiator is to ask people for the best way to reach them. Most real estate professionals do not even ask for an e-mail address, let alone the best way to reach a person. Effective communication is important to you so you want to know the best way to reach your client. For many today, that method is not the telephone, but e-mail. Asking these questions says something positive to those clients and customers who are e-mail communicators. Here are several suggestions of places to collect e-mail addresses.

1. Ask for e-mail addresses at the open house. Create a column in your open house guest register. Often people are reluctant to give you a phone number but they may be less reluctant to give you an e-mail address. When someone does give you an e-mail address at an open house, they have, in effect, told you what type of property they are interested in, the neighborhood they are interested in, the price range, the architecture, etc. You can now drop this e-mail address into your automated MLS search and communication functionality, providing the prospect with new listings when they are entered into the MLS database, which, of course, puts your name in front of them one more time (you can't put your name in front of people too many times in this business). Consider adding a statement to your open house log stating that if a visitor leaves his or her e-mail address that you will then provide them with similar property listing information until they ask not to receive it any longer.

2. Use your voice mail. Change your voice mail message to ask for a return telephone number, a return e-mail address, and the best way to reach the caller. Again, just asking says something about you. Remember, it is the little things, all added up, that make the difference.

3. If your office has a receptionist, train your receptionist to ask for e-mail addresses of callers. It is a little thing, but it is the little things that make a difference.

FIGURE 8.1 ■ Adding E-Mail Addresses to Your Contacts List

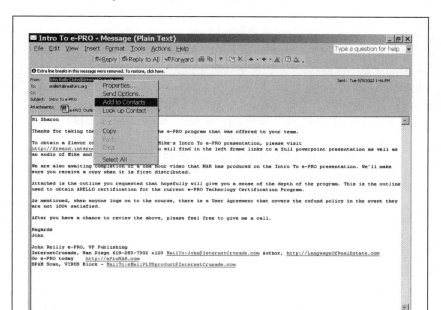

Screen shot reprinted by permission from Microsoft Corporation.

Start collecting e-mail addresses now. It is as easy as a **right click.** The right click method will also avoid misspellings as you transfer information into the address book. In Windows-compatible software, whenever an e-mail comes in, place the cursor over the name of the person in the header and click the right mouse button to open the menu for that item. One of the selections will be similar to "Add to Contacts." This will place the information into your address book.

Other people are using this method to put your e-mail address into their e-mail address book. You want to make sure that the return address set in your e-mail software is the one you want people to have—your permanent e-mail address.

One way to insert someone's e-mail address into your e-mail address book is to right click on an e-mail address.

From the drop down menu, select "Add to Contacts" and the following window will appear:

Click on "Save and Close" and the e-mail address and name of sender are now part of your e-mail address book.

FIGURE 8.2 ■ Contact Information Page

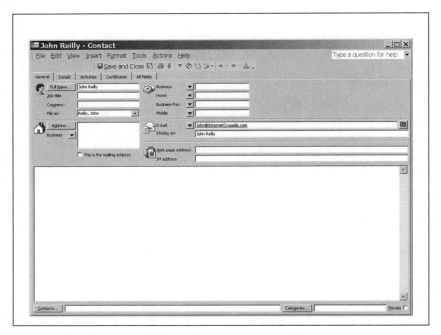

Screen shot reprinted by permission from Microsoft Corporation.

■ IMPORTANCE OF PROMPTNESS WHEN REPLYING TO E-MAIL

Often those interested in your services are interested in an immediate response—they may have seen your listing online and would like to see the property right away. For that reason, you will want to be online whenever you are in the office, at home, or even on the road. Checking your e-mail at least as often as you check your voice mail is at the heart of being a new real estate professional. Those who are e-mailing you are oftentimes computer professionals who receive and send e-mail throughout the day. If you delay in getting back to them, you may miss an opportunity.

In many instances, all you need to do to differentiate yourself from your competition and get the listing is to reply to your e-mail.

■ FUNDAMENTAL ELEMENTS OF AN E-MAIL MARKETING STRATEGY

It's the little things that make a difference. Each of the following elements can be implemented individually. You need not use all of the elements to get the benefits of any one of the individual elements you implement. The **synergy** does increase with each additional element you implement. Even adding a few of these will be good for your real estate practice now and will prove even more beneficial a year or two down the road.

- Understand the features and functionality available in a mail account and make sure your mail account offers unlimited e-mail addresses and an **auto reply** feature. Unlimited e-mail addresses are useful for e-mail addresses on the fly, for advertising, and for tracking (maintaining your privacy). Decide if the auto reply feature fits your style of dealing with e-mail. Uses include a vacation message and a **confirmation message.**
- Use your domain in your e-mail address to create a true permanent e-mail address.
- Change your return address in your e-mail software to reflect your permanent e-mail address.
- Create an auto-signature in your e-mail software (use embedded links). Consider using the auto-signature feature for information you send out on a repetitive basis, such as agency disclousure.
- Set up your e-mail filing system by creating a folder for every listing and every transaction. Create a folder for each person you receive e-mail from on a frequent basis and need to refer to occasionally.
- Collect e-mail addresses from everyone you meet. Part of the problem with e-mail addresses is that they change frequently for many people. As a real estate professional, wouldn't it be nice if your e-mail address book always had the current e-mail addresses of all your contacts? If all your contacts had permanent e-mail addresses, it would. What does it take to have a permanent e-mail address? Your own domain and e-mail forwarding.
- When communicating to your entire e-mail database in a single e-mail message, create an e-mail address for the list using the unlimited e-mail address feature such as VIPList@YourName.com; put it in the "To" field; and place the rest of the e-mail addresses (populated from a group in your e-mail soft-

ware) in the Bcc field. This will protect the identity of those in your database and looks better than "undisclosed recipients" in the header of an e-mail message.

- Use mail merge software or the combination of Outlook and Word to send personalized e-mail. This requires learning the functionality in the software—not an insurmountable task. You can pay to have someone else do this for you, but always maintain control of your database.
- Use a Web-based listserv as a one-way newsletter. In all cases, use embedded links to access your online newsletter, if you have one; any published information you have on the Web; and your Web site.
- Use auto-responders (e-mail embedded links)
- Be consistent. Once you begin regular communication with your e-mail database, keep it up; consistency will pay off.
- Participate in online communities to build a presence with other real estate professionals and with consumers.
- Create your own online communities with listservs and with **bulletin board** and **chat** functionality.

Real estate is a people business, and every day real estate professionals are networking and meeting people. The Internet is the network of networks and offers great opportunity for the real estate professional willing to create a presence in different online communities. One way to do this, yet untapped, is to participate on the local bulletin boards of the national listing **aggregator** real estate sites. Post relevant neighborhood information and crosspost your content for maximum exposure. You will, as the public becomes aware of the information, become known and gain a presence on that bulletin board. Answers to questions you write and the information you post on local points of interest can also be published in your e-mail and Web marketing pieces. Remember, connected consumers are looking for speed, convenience, choice, value-added, quality, service, discounts, and information.

FUNDAMENTALS OF EFFECTIVE E-MAIL-BASED MARKETING

You will reach more people more frequently with e-mail at this stage of the development of the Internet than you will by having people visit your Web site. This is a money-saving concept as Web site services are much more costly than e-mail services. Where is the first place most people check when they go online and where do people spend most of their online time? The answer is their e-mail inbox in their e-mail software.

As you define and implement your personal e-mail marketing program, you will see that properly cultivated Internet leads turn into buyers or sellers.

Real estate is a business of relationships, and relationships are built upon communication. E-mail offers a new

■ **TIP**
If you want to reach people on the Internet, don't wait for them to go to your Web site —get into their inbox.

dimension of communication and a new concept of documentation for most people. An ongoing e-mail communication marketing program will give you the opportunity to demonstrate expertise and build trust and confidence with your client base. There is so much more to e-mail than "send and receive."

Communication and documentation are at the heart of real estate transactions. Increasing one's knowledge of e-mail—how it works, how it doesn't work, and how others use it—is a key to success in the age of information. The real estate business is a business where relationships, referrals, and return business are the result of constant client contact. E-mail affords everyone the ability to reach more people more often with fewer resources than required by previous methods of communication. Can you remember a time when you noticed a past client had listed with someone else? Perhaps you were not in their mind and weren't marketing to them enough. E-mail can easily fill that void!

The degree to which you take advantage of e-mail is up to you and will be directly measurable in dollars to your bottom line.

INTERNET NEWSLETTER MARKETING

Many professionals have built their business on the basis of continuous and repetitive communication with their prospect base. A prospect base is usually broken down as to prospects, current clients, and past clients. A printed newsletter, distributed monthly or even weekly, often facilitates this communication. For some, this requires investment in high-quality color printed material. Many real estate professionals pay someone else to write the newsletters, some hiring a service to manage the whole effort from start to finish.

E-mail and automated e-mail software make it almost too easy to produce high-quality newsletters on a regular basis, at little cost. We say "almost too easy" to emphasize that it might be tempting to send these newsletters too frequently or to those who would rather not receive them. The recommended practice is to send them to people who opt in to your newsletter. Yes, it is acceptable to send once as an invitation to opt in, but after that you are sending unsolicited e-mail—spam. Avoid, at all costs, sending e-mail to those who have opted out! Be sure to follow federal and state law on anti-spam requirements.

Make a commitment to create a periodic communication to your database via e-mail with information the recipients may find valuable (example: the increase in the median price of homes in the neighborhood). The more valuable the information, the less you will see your base opting out.

This information can be sent to a general list, using Web-based Listserv software. With today's ISPs clamping down on authentication and other restrictions to reduce spam, the Listserv is becoming a more popular alternative for mass e-mailings by real estate professionals.

Personalized communications can be sent using e-mail merge software. Each e-mail would be addressed: "Dear (name of client)."

Another technique is to combine a Web newsletter format with an e-mail form of delivery. Companies offer Web solutions that you can customize. Include the URL of your Web newsletter in all your e-mail and other marketing pieces.

With today's increasing usage of Web editor software (FrontPage, DreamWeaver, etc.), it is becoming easier to create your own compelling newsletter Web pages. Even Microsoft Word can perform the task. These can then be linked to or from an e-mail message, printed and distributed like flyers, or saved to a disk or CD-ROM for handout. Given the graphical nature of Web pages, it is easy to add dramatic images, colors, and more—creating a super-powerful message for your market.

http://InternetNewsletters.RealTown.com

MASS MAILINGS

Once per quarter, consider sending an e-mail communication to your database. There are many ways you can accomplish this goal. For example, you can use an e-mail merge software such as World Merge (downloadable at *http://www.coloradosoft.com/worldmrg/*); or, you can use a combination of Microsoft Word to create the message and Microsoft Outlook to send it.

Which software is the best? The one you use.

Make sure your e-mail communications contain embedded links to information such as Virtual Tours, Web Newsletter, and Neighborhood News.

Staying in front of your sphere of influence year after year is the secret of success for many real estate professionals. E-mail, properly utilized, will ensure a steady return of repeat and referral business. As most of your clients will only need your services every five to eight years (on average), it is important to maintain consistent contact over long periods of time. E-mail marketing allows you a way to provide valuable information in a cost-effective manner. Homeowners like to be kept up to date on what is taking place in their neighborhood and community. They are interested in information about:

- what's for sale and what just sold;
- business moving to or contemplating moving into the area;
- garage sales;
- new zoning or proposed zoning and/or political agendas;
- interest rate changes;
- favorable tax law changes;
- new and interesting info on the Internet;
- high school sports schedules; and
- Little League schedules.

Make sure, however, to provide a visible means for the recipients to opt out of these mailings. Usually, a statement such as "You are receiving this message as a courtesy to my friends and clients. In the event you do not wish to receive these mailings in the future, please reply to this message with 'Remove' in the subject line."

Web-based Listservs are gaining in popularity as ISPs continue in their efforts to clamp down on spam by limiting mass e-mailings, even legitimate opt-in mailings.

The following are suggestions for optimizing use of e-mail:

1. Purchase your own domain; act now to acquire your own domain name before someone else grabs it.
2. Use your own domain in your e-mail addresses and in your Web site address (URL).

3. Use the signature feature in your e-mail software and include a) name and designations (like e-PRO, CRS, ABR); b) Web site address (be sure to include the http:// prefix); c) e-mail address (include the mailto: prefix with no space); d) phone number and fax number; and e) your state, city, or town for possible referrals.
4. Use multiple signatures for different spheres of influence and online communities with which you participate. Remember, any report or information you send repetitively can be built into the signature feature.
5. Use a permanent e-mail address, You@You.com. This can be acquired for the cost of an E-mail forwarding account, which is about $69 per year.
6. Make sure you are using a return e-mail address that reflects your domain and not the domain of your ISP.
7. Learn more about auto responders: how they can be used with your domain, and how they will provide instant feedback to interested parties, and, at the same time, send you the e-mail addresses of the interested parties.
8. Build your e-mail address book. Ask everyone you meet for their e-mail address. Ask for e-mail addresses in all your correspondence, at open houses, on your voice mail message—everywhere you can think of. To market electronically, you will need to capture e-mail addresses.
9. Understand that it is in your best interest for everyone to have a permanent e-mail address. That way your e-mail address book will always be up-to-date.
10. Set up a list newsletter and begin to communicate with your sphere of influence in a cost-effective manner.
11. Make sure your spell check is on when composing e-mail. Remember, *every piece of e-mail is a marketing piece.* You only have one chance to make a first impression.
12. Begin to use Third Level Domains in your e-mail marketing and at least on your sold properties (*Sold.YourName.com*).

Do it now. Don't wait; get the competitive edge on your competition. If you are interested in InternetCrusade's Web and e-mail services, please drop an e-mail, give a call, or send a blank e-mail to this auto responder: ProductInfo@InternetCrusade.com.

Chapter Links:
http://InternetNewsletters.RealTown.com

■ REVIEW QUESTIONS

1. (T/F) Asking for and collecting e-mail addresses is the first step in creating an e-mail marketing plan.

   Answer: True.

   Ask for e-mail addresses at every opportunity. Just asking for someone's e-mail address says something positive about you to Internet users and will differentiate you from your competition.

2. (T/F) E-mail offers a new dimension of communication and a new concept of documentation for most people.

   Answer: True.

   Communication and documentation are at the heart of real estate transactions. Increasing one's knowledge of e-mail—how it works, how it doesn't work, and how others use it—is a key to success in the age of information.

3. How does the Outlook software differ from the Outlook Express software?

   Answer: In Outlook you can store and retrieve detailed information about each contact; you can also link those contacts to activities, appointments, files, messages, and other journal-style information. In this regard, Outlook Express is simply an e-mail manager. Outlook is a full-fledged contact and e-mailing system, which is also known as a PIM (Personal Information Manager) or personal productivity software.

Chapter Nine

E-Mail Security and E-Mail Viruses

Opportunity never knocks; it is within you.
DENIS WAITLEY
http://Motivation.RealTown.com

Although it is true that much of the buzz surrounding viruses on the Internet is the result of media hype and panic, there is also the very real dark side of the Internet where viruses live every day. Your system, files, and e-mail are all vulnerable to attack; and you can easily find yourself out of luck and on the receiving end of a viral attack unless you know how and take the steps needed to protect yourself and your files. Viruses can make your computer vulnerable to future attack, open your computer for use by others, or just simply destroy your **hard drive.**

E-mail-borne viruses are clogging up the Internet, slowing down e-mail delivery, and devouring untold amounts of human productivity. Moreover, this is just the tip of the iceberg, not taking into consideration dangerous "worms" that can destroy hardware and software and compromise security and privacy. That's another story.

Today's e-mail viruses have the ability to spoof the "From" and "Subject" fields of an e-mail message, disguising the sender's e-mail address, which prevents you from knowing who really sent the virus.

Familiar names are now a dangerous decoy, luring you into a false sense of security and tempting you to open virus-infected e-mail. Because the "From" field is spoofed, you may be falsely accused of spreading a virus and also receive numerous e-mails you did not request.

■ THE PROCESS OF INFECTION

What takes place when a virus-infected e-mail is sent?

An e-mail with a virus attached is generally sent:

- to someone who does not have antivirus software on his or her computer;
- to someone who has antivirus software on their computer but has not updated by downloading the latest virus definitions and installing them;
- to someone before the antivirus software companies have created the cure for a recently released virus.

The virused e-mail is opened (or viewed through the preview pane) and infects the recipient's computer. The virus then:

- creates an e-mail message (not detectable in the outbox) on the newly infected computer;
- pulls an e-mail address at random out of the e-mail address book of the newly infected computer and puts it in the "From" field of the newly created e-mail message (spoofs the "From" field);
- puts some text in the subject field;
- attaches a copy of the virus to the newly created e-mail message; and
- sends the e-mail with the virus attached to many of the addresses in the address book of the newly infected computer.

The following results: The virus is received by those to whom it is sent and the cycle above begins again. Moreover, those who receive the virus may think that the virus was sent by the spoofed e-mail address in the "From" field. Remember, the person in the "From" field did not send the virus.

Some of the virus protection software on the computers to which the new virused e-mail message was sent detects the virus and is set (a setting in the antivirus software) to send a response to the e-mail address in the "From" field when it detects (and fixes, deletes, or quarantines) a virus.

When this happens, the e-mail that states "A virus has been sent by you" is being sent to someone who did not send the virus (misdirected because of the spoofed "From" field"). This is why you may be receiving

FIGURE 9.1 ■ Virus Protection Software

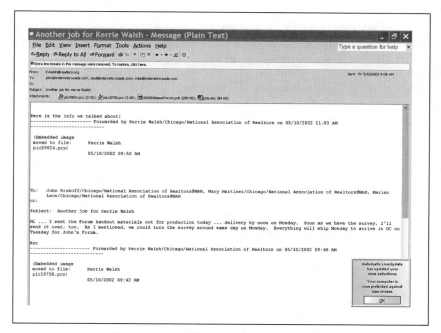

Screen shot reprinted by permission from Microsoft Corporation.

e-mail messages that say you have sent a virus, and you know you did not. You did not send a virus but your e-mail address was the e-mail address that appeared in the "From" field of an e-mail message with a virus attached.

You may also receive auto responders you did not request. If your e-mail address is in the "From" field of an e-mail message sent to an auto-responder, you will receive the auto-response event though you did not request it. If your e-mail address is in the "From" field, it doesn't matter that you did not send the request; the auto responder thinks you sent it.

What can you do? It is best to follow these suggestions:

1. Keep your virus protection software updated with the latest virus definitions. Put the software in "automatic" so when new virus definitions are available, the software company's servers will detect the next time you are online and update your computer automatically, notifying you of the update after the update is complete.

There are several antivirus products on the market today. Two surface as the most widely used: McAfee and Norton. McAfee offers both traditional **shrink-wrapped** software solutions as well as the online Web-accessible *McAfee.com.* In each case you can pay an annual fee to maintain access to the latest virus definitions.

http://AntiVirusSoftware.RealTown.com

2. Run a complete virus scan on a regular basis as well as if you ever suspect that you have a virus.
3. Don't open attachments unless you are expecting them; if so, you may want to check with the sender before you open the attachment just to make sure the sender sent it to you.
4. Realize that using the preview pane option may make you more susceptible to actually being infected by one of the many viruses you will inevitably receive (and have already been receiving). This is just a caution, as the preview pane is a very convenient way to sort through large volumes of e-mail; should you opt to use it, however, just understand the potential for infection and the need to keep your antivirus software up to date. You might also consider creating a folder for attachments in your e-mail software and a rule that filters any e-mail with an attachment into the attachment folder. Use the preview pane in your inbox folder and turn off the preview pane in your attachment folder. Your ability to have the preview pane availability set differently in different folders is a function of the version of the e-mail software you are using.
5. Turn off the feature in your antivirus software that automatically sends out an e-mail to the e-mail address in the "From" folder of a virused e-mail—that feature likely is sending the notification to the wrong person. For all practical purposes, you will not be able to tell from whom the virused e-mail originated.
6. Consider a server side e-mail product that helps eliminate viruses at the server before they reach your computer.
7. Inform your clients of the information provided here so they don't someday think you sent them a virus. If your e-mail address is in the e-mail address books of others, there is a good chance that someday your e-mail address will appear in the "From" field of an infected e-mail and some of the recipients who do not understand the nature of today's e-mail viruses will think you sent them a virus.

Computer viruses are a fact of life, but there is much you can do to minimize their risk to you and your productivity.

Important Note: Do not open file attachments from an unknown source. Do not run executable files that have been attached to e-mail and sent to you—even if you know and trust the sender! This is how viruses are spread through e-mail. Often the virus will replicate itself by attacking the sender's e-mail system. The virus then grabs many addresses from the address book (people you know) and sends an innocent-looking message with an executable (.exe, .vbs, .com, or .bat file extensions) attachment. When the attachment is opened, the virus is activated, going into the recipient's address book, and then repeating the process.

Invest in a personal firewall if you are on an always on broadband connection. Cable and DSL users—this is a must! This can help protect you from such attacks from **backdoor viruses.**

The best course of action when you realize you have sent a virus is to contact everyone in your address book, letting them know you have unintentionally sent them a virus and not to open the e-mail or the attachment sent by you. Anyone who has opened the virus-infected file sent by you should notify everyone in their address book, as the virus has probably spread through them like it was through you. In your e-mail, be sure to include a link to Symantec (Norton) or McAfee where they can find instructions on how to treat the virus.

The following is a sample of e-mail to be sent to all e-mail addresses in your address book when you realize you have spread a computer virus:

To: Everyone in your e-mail address book
From: You
Subject: DO NOT OPEN E-MAIL ATTACHMENT SENT FROM ME! Virus Notification

I am sorry for the inconvenience. I have unintentionally sent you a file containing the Snow White Virus. Do not open any e-mail attachment from me.

If you opened the attachment and you have not recently updated your antivirus software, the Snow White Virus has probably infected your computer and sent the virus out to everyone in your address book, as it did with mine.

If this is the case, please copy and paste this letter in a new e-mail message and send it to everyone in your address book.

For more information on the Snow White Virus and the best way to treat your computer go to *http://McAfee.com*.

Once again, I am sorry for the great inconvenience.

Yours Truly,

In the above e-mail, make sure that *http://McAffee.com* is an **embedded link.**

Because of the nature of viruses today, if your e-mail address is in someone else's e-mail address book, you will at some point be accused of sending a virus. When this happens, the following explanation can be sent to the accuser:

Dear _____:

Today's viruses have the ability to spoof the "From" and "Subject" fields of an e-mail message, which prevents you from knowing who really sent you the virus or the content of the e-mail.

Familiar names are now a dangerous decoy, luring you into a false sense of security and tempting you to open infected e-mail. Be careful and keep your virus protection software updated with the latest virus definitions. I try to update daily (it takes only seconds) and have my Norton antivirus software set to run automatic updates (instead of asking me if I want to update).

Run a complete virus scan if you ever suspect that you have a virus. I have my computer set to scan on a regular basis.

It might be a good idea to inform your clients of the above so they don't someday think you sent them a virus.

If your e-mail address is in the e-mail address books of others, there is a good chance that someday your e-mail address will appear in the "From" field of an infected e-mail and some of the recipients who do not understand the nature of today's e-mail viruses will think you sent them a virus.

Sincerely,

Your name

■ BEWARE OF VIRUS HOAXES

Virus hoaxes can often be as annoying as viruses themselves and are a sign of the inexperienced user. Before you send a letter to friends and business associates apologizing for sending a virus, make sure that you in fact were infected with a computer virus. Update your virus definitions and run a virus scan. Also check out the different hoaxes at:

http://VirusesandHoaxes.RealTown.com

■ BACKING UP YOUR FILES

You will remember the last time you backed up the moment you need the backup. You have a lot of time and energy invested in your files and for that reason you want to protect them should your computer crash or be stolen.

When you back up, you make a copy of your files on another memory medium. This could be a floppy disk, Zip drive, CD, or tape drive (depending on the size of the files you are backing up). It is a good practice to test your backups occasionally to ensure solid backup with no corrupted files. It is also good practice to keep your backup in a different location, away from your computer.

http://Backup.RealTown.com

Chapter Links:
http://AntiVirusSoftware.RealTown.com
http://VirusesandHoaxes.RealTown.com
http://Backup.RealTown.com

■ REVIEW QUESTIONS

1. (T/F) Today's e-mail viruses have the ability to spoof the "From" and "Subject" fields of an e-mail message, which prevents you from knowing who really sent you the virus.

    Answer: True

    Familiar names are now a dangerous decoy, luring you into a false sense of security and tempting you to open virus-infected e-mail. Because the "From" field is spoofed, you may be falsely accused of spreading a virus and also receive numerous e-mails you did not request.

2. What are some of the things you can do to protect your computer from virus attack?

   Answer: Have the latest version of antivirus software, updated with the latest antivirus definitions.

   Run a complete virus scan if you ever suspect that you have a virus and on a regular basis as well.

   Don't open attachments unless you are expecting them; you may want to check with the sender before you open the attachment just to make sure he or she sent it to you.

   Realize that using the preview pane option may make you more susceptible to actually being infected by one of the many viruses you will inevitably receive (and have already been receiving).

3. (T/F) Virus hoaxes can often be as annoying as viruses themselves and are a sign of the inexperienced user.

   Answer: True.

   Before you send a letter to friends and business associates apologizing for sending a virus, make sure that you in fact were infected with a computer virus. Update your virus definitions and run a virus scan.

Chapter Ten

The World Wide Web . . .

In the Beginning

Positive self-direction is the action plan that all winners in life use to turn imagination into reality, fantasy into fact, and dreams into actual goals.

DENIS WAITLEY
http://Motivation.RealTown.com

■ HISTORY OF THE WORLD WIDE WEB (WWW)

The World Wide Web (WWW) is a fairly recent phenomenon that offers a new advertising, marketing, and publishing vehicle to anyone with content and a few hundred dollars. It was, however, not created with marketing in mind. The first proposal for the WWW was made at CERN (the European Organization for Nuclear Research), the world's largest particle physics center, by Tim Berners-Lee in 1989, and further refined in 1990. The Web was originally conceived and developed to meet the demand for information sharing between scientists working in different universities and institutes around the world. For a review of the history of the WWW, go to the birthplace of the Web, CERN.

http://BirthOfTheWeb.RealTown.com

■ REAL ESTATE AND THE WWW

Real estate Web sites started to appear on the WWW as **brochure ware** in 1995 and have evolved since then. The Web site of the real estate professional who successfully markets and services consumers today is a real estate Web site that contains rich content, the most important of which is information on current available listing inventory.

Initially, **home pages** (as they were first called) were created in a programming language called HTML (hypertext mark-up language, still used today). To build a Web site required that you either studied HTML yourself or hired a programmer (and sometimes a graphic designer) to build the site for you.

Software companies such as Microsoft have created Web editing software that allows the user to create web pages in what might be called a **WYSIWYG** (What You See Is What You Get) format. Users create pages either in familiar word processing layouts or in newer drag-and-drop layouts where you simply drop items (text, images, and so on) onto the page where you want the items located. The software takes care of creating the HTML and other code required to make the site work.

Web editing software makes it easier for people to build Web sites. You don't have to learn HTML, but you do have to learn to use the Web editing software. The "buy or build" decision for most real estate professionals should be based on the effective use of their time. Is it more cost-effective for you to do what you do best—sell real estate—or take the time to learn how to program so you can build your own Web site?

In 1996, listings from across the country began to appear on the Internet, aggregated in largest number at *REALTOR.com. REALTOR.com* was, at the time, owned entirely by a wholly owned subsidiary of the National Association of REALTORS® (NAR), the REALTORS® Information Network, RIN. *(http://RIN.RealTown.com)*

Homestore, Inc., a publicly traded Internet company, now operates *REALTOR.com,* subject to a management agreement in which NAR retains ownership of the REALTOR® logo and the *REALTOR.com* site name. In addition, NAR is a minority shareholder in Homestore (HOMS–NASDAQ) and has representation on the board of directors.

By contracting directly with the Multiple Listing Services across the country, *REALTOR.com* became the largest **aggregator** of listing information on the Internet, and as such attracted (and continues to draw) huge numbers of consumers to the *REALTOR.com* Web site.

■ THE WEB IS INFORMATION

A Web site is an important aspect of the overall marketing plan for the real estate professional. Your Web site is a growing part of your Web presence on the Internet. Just as having a business card is fundamental for real estate professionals, a Web site is becoming equally important.

More consumers are going to the Web to find information about real estate and real estate professionals before they make direct personal contact. If you haven't experienced this yourself, it is just a matter of time. The National Association of REALTORS® 2003 Survey of homebuyers and sellers indicates that 71 percent of those with Web access use the Internet to assist them *(http://NARSurvey.RealTown.com)*. To compete in the online world, real estate professionals must create a Web site that gives them the ability to control and maintain the content, anticipate what information their audience will want, and then provide it in a manner that is compelling and easy to use.

You must know what consumers expect from the Web. Read and learn. Ask and listen. Whenever you encounter someone who has looked for real estate information on the Web, be an information sponge! Ask them how they found the sites they visited. Try to find out what specific words and phrases they used in their searches. In short, find out what they were looking for and use that information to make certain that they and others will find you in the future!

> ## ■ TIP
> Develop a Web site with content that will appeal to individuals even when they are not interested in buying and selling real estate. For example, if you are prospecting a condo project, have information such as the CC & Rs, articles of incorporation, bylaws, pool rules, etc., available at your Web site and let everyone who lives in that condo project know that if they need that information, your Web site is the place to find it.

■ RECOGNIZING THE POTENTIAL USES OF THE WEB

One of the first questions you must ask yourself when considering your Web strategy is, "What is a Web site going to do for me?" Web sites can serve many purposes. A Web site can be as simple as the family photo album or as complex as an online product purchase, delivery, and support network. It can be a marketing brochure or a virtual community. So many possibilities are being recognized daily that it becomes almost impossible to come up with a defined list of uses for what is referred to as a Web site.

Web sites can be brochure ware, where you can tell the world about yourself, your area, and your services—an electronic billboard. Current uses of the Web for the real estate industry run from the simple property brochure to the complex member-only password-protected sites (such as *REALTOR.org*).

For real estate professionals, Web sites can be a publishing vehicle, providing information to the homebuying and selling public. Web sites can be community gathering spots—a place to share and learn with other professionals.

Web sites can be information-passing Intranets, such as those offered by major franchises to keep their sales staff current with new forms, company policy, and educational training.

> **■ TIP**
> Community-created content draws Web site visitors. Include on your Web site an area for members of your community to publish information of interest to them.

■ FUTURE OF WEB SITES

Many technological advances relying on the Web have received lukewarm receptions. Business-to-consumer retailing on the Web, business-to-business marketing, application service providers (ASP), and free Internet access supported by ads all are on the downward slide.

An absolute fact, however, is that the Internet is the fastest-growing technology in modern times. Current projects are underway to create major online transaction management tools specific to the real estate industry. The thinking is that the more documents and schedule-consuming items pertaining to the transaction that can be moved to electronic communication and management, the faster the transaction can be done. Once these tools are in wide use, it is guesstimated that the typical residential transaction can be whittled down to a few days. This is perhaps five to ten years down the road.

A licensee's Web site content should relate not only to information necessary in the real estate sales cycle, but also to information that consumers can use on a regular basis, whether or not they currently are in the market for real estate. If a Web site contains this type of information, the consumer may return to the site when there is no need for real estate sales services. You will in effect be in front of consumers on a more regular basis. If consumers visit your site more frequently than every five to eight years, you win. This is the key to any successful advertising and marketing program.

Real estate sales professionals often give away promotional items that have nothing to do with real estate. They often give away premium items to keep their name in front of people (prospects)—items such as customized note pads, calendars, pens, rain caps, flyswatters, refrigerator magnets, and other "tools of the trade" paraphernalia. Now, one of the premiums you can offer consumers is information—made available conveniently on a Web site. Information is the currency of the 21st century, and real estate is an information-based business and service.

When there is enough consumer demand, we will see more real estate professionals offering secured areas for client transaction-related documentation, from contracts to loan documents. It is not too early to look at this eventuality as you consider your Web strategy, what you expect your Web site to do for you, and how that fits into your overall marketing plan and your marketing budget.

Chapter Links:
http://BirthOfTheWeb.RealTown.com
http://RIN.RealTown.com

■ REVIEW QUESTIONS

1. (T/F) Developing a Web site is a costly proposition.

   Answer: False.

   The World Wide Web is a fairly recent phenomenon that offers a new advertising, marketing, and publishing vehicle to anyone with content and a few hundred dollars.

2. (T/F) The World Wide Web was created as an inexpensive way to market goods and services.

   Answer: False.

   The Web was originally conceived and developed to meet the demand for information sharing between scientists working in different universities and institutes around the world.

3. (T/F) Real estate professionals need not be concerned with the development of the Web as it pertains to its use in the real estate

transaction, from the finding of the property to the closing and transfer of title.

Answer: False.

To compete in the online world, real estate professionals must create a Web site that gives them the ability to control and maintain the content, anticipate what information their audience will want, and then provide it in a manner that is compelling and easy to use.

Chapter Eleven

The World Wide Web (WWW)—
Web Sites Are Billboards in the Middle of Nowhere

Perfection is devastated by failure, while excellence learns from failure.
DENIS WAITLEY
http://Motivation.RealTown.com

Once your e-mail marketing plan is in place, you will want to take the next step and decide how the World Wide Web will help you achieve your overall Internet marketing objectives. The WWW is the graphical part of the Internet with easy to use, point-and-click navigation. The software utilized for viewing the World Wide Web is a browser, the most widely used browser being Microsoft's Internet Explorer, which comes with most computers as an integral part of the Microsoft **Windows Operating System.**

http://InternetExplorer.RealTown.com

■ USING A WEB SITE FOR MARKETING, PUBLISHING, SERVICE, AND SUPPORT

An Internet presence is made up of an e-mail presence and a **Web presence** and, just as your domain is the foundation of your e-mail presence (You@Your-Name.com), your domain is the center of your Web presence as well. The address of your Web site, the URL (Uniform

> ### ■ TIP
> Make sure your Web site address and your e-mail address both reflect your domain.

Resource Locator), should contain your domain (http://Your-Name.com). Your domain host (remember, there are three types of Internet hosts—domain host, e-mail host, Web host) will point your domain to your Web site, no matter who your Web host might be.

Keep in mind that Web sites are billboards in the middle of nowhere and this must be an ever-present consideration as you contemplate the purchase of a Web site. Since the commercialization of the browser in 1994, real estate professionals have wasted hundreds of millions of dollars on Web sites nobody visits. It is essential that you develop a Web site strategy in addition to having a Web site. Having a Web site with no Web site strategy is like throwing your money into a bottomless pit.

Many real estate professionals are searching for that magic Web site that comes up in the top ten of search engines, and brings them more local and out-of-area referral business than they can handle. That magic Web site does not exist. A successful Web site requires a well thought-out consistent application (based on criteria such as budget and audience) of Internet marketing strategies (both e-mail and the Web) over a relatively long period of time. Having a Web strategy will help yield the best results from a Web site as you work to get the most return from the money you allocate to Internet marketing.

What is your Web strategy? For many real estate professionals the answer is to buy another Web site, acquire a clever URL, pay someone to get the site ranked in certain search engines, and then hope the leads will come rolling in. The real estate professionals who employ these strategies will end up looking like Rip Van Winkle before they can live on the commissions generated from such a plan.

The better strategy and the one that will have a greater likelihood of consistent success begins with research into the objectives, tools, and mindset of the target audience coupled with a review of Web sites of other successful real estate professionals. After conducting this research, you will be better able to make an informed decision about what your site should be, what it should cost, and how much you can realistically expect to gain from allocating marketing dollars to this endeavor.

■ DEVELOPING YOUR WEB SITE

In many cases, a consumer's first exposure to you, your services, and your abilities is your Web site. Your Web site is you to the visitor. It is the first impression of you, and as the saying goes, "You only have one opportunity to make a good first impression."

Your Web site is a publishing vehicle and must include information about you, your company, property listings, and specific information about the community in which you work.

PLANNING YOUR WEB SITE

Real estate professionals are investing in Web sites for no apparent reason other than everyone else is doing it. Many brokers and salespeople fail to develop a strategy for their Web site. Often they purchase the first solution they are shown, only to be unhappy with the results, not to mention poorer. When considering what you want your Web site to be and do for you, your prospects, customers, and clients, it is important to make sure that your offering is at least as helpful to your audience as your competitor's Web site. If possible, make your Web site a little bit more interesting, more useful—something to make your site different. Remember that it's the little things that make a difference.

Before you invest your time and money in a Web site, gain an understanding of the Internet and the World Wide Web. It is true in all business investments and it is true with Web sites as well—investing your time before investing your money usually pays handsome rewards. Your knowledge of what consumers are seeing at your competitor's Web site is important to you. What functionality and graphics are your competitors using? Explore the Internet (surf); look at other real estate professional and broker Web sites. Know what your competition is doing on the Web.

One way to find Web site addresses of your competitors is to go to a search engine such as *Google.com*, then type in the name of your city and the words "real estate." This should give you plenty of Web sites to review. You might also just type in the name of your competitor in the search field and see what comes up.

■ **TIP**

Conduct a Web site survey of your competition. Go to Google.com and search for your most successful competitors by name.

Web Site Survey Checklist:

1. Determine the five market leaders in your area. This information is usually obtainable through your MLS.

2. Go to *Google.com* and enter their names (conduct a separate search for each).
3. With the search results, visit the Web sites of the market leaders,
4. Record the following for each of their Web sites:
   A. Colors
   B. Content (listings, theirs, much of the MLS, national)
   C. Design and ease of navigation
   D. Do they contain Privacy Policies?
   E. Is their e-mail address on each page?
   F. Any outstanding features you liked
   G. Is there a method for collecting e-mail addresses?
   H. What did you like about the Web sites you visited?
   I. What didn't you like?
   J. Were the sites quick to load?
   K. What information on the site is helpful to prospective buyers and sellers?
   L. What information on the site is helpful to current clients under contract?
   M. Is the salesperson or broker displaying his or her own domain in the URL of the Web site?
   N. Is there an option on every page to e-mail to the site owner?
   O. Does the e-mail, when opened on the site, display the e-mail address with the same domain of the site?
   P. Was there any other information on the site you found useful or interesting?

Once again, a Web site must be part of an Internet marketing plan, which should be part of an overall marketing plan. An Internet marketing plan requires the creation of an e-mail presence and a Web presence. Keep in mind that Internet marketing is not stand-alone marketing. Internet marketing must be integrated into traditional marketing methods to achieve results.

SEARCH ENGINES AND BEHIND-THE-SCENES CONTENT—META-TAGS

Do you ever wonder how sites end up listed in **search engines** like Yahoo or Google? Search engines usually look at the **meta-tags** in your site, the site title, and the actual content on your pages. This is where you can make a difference, albeit a small one.

Make sure that you have enough of the right phraseology within your content. Words such as "homes" and "houses" become critically important. Next, make sure to have a good set of meta-tags in the header of each page of your site. If you are working with a site designer, let them know the list of tags you expect to have on each page; then make sure that these words are actually coded into your pages. These tags should be descriptive of what is presented on that page. If you are going it alone—designing your own site—you should have a clear understanding of what meta-tags are and how they work for you.

Simply put, meta data is data about a document—in this case, information about your Web site. These tags must be constructed in a very precise way, but they also should contain imprecise data (misspellings and more).

Search engines crawling the Web looking for words like "realty," "homes," "houses," and so on will notice the page containing these meta-tag words. You need to know that the search engines are wise to some of the trickery in use—such things as repeated meta words and invisible text no longer work. Invisible text is text on a page that is the same color as the page background, making it invisible to the eye but not to the Web-crawling search engine. Also, the maximum character count for each meta-tag is 128 characters. So be wise with the use of your meta-tags and content embedded in your Web pages.

If high ranking is important to you, consider retaining a search engine optimization specialist who will spend the time keeping current with the rapid changes in the search rules—while you are spending your time practicing your real estate skills.

LOCAL WEB HOSTING VERSUS NATIONAL WEB HOSTING— CUSTOMER SERVICE IS THE KEY

Local hosting companies are not necessarily the best companies to host your Web site. You want your Web site hosted on the fastest servers possible and you want good service for the price you pay. Your domain (*You.com* or *YourBrand.com*) is the center of your Web presence. When checking and comparing Web hosts, print their services and their fees so you can easily compare host to host.

> **■ TIP**
> Make sure your domain host sets up the domain records properly to allow access with or without the "www" in your Web site address.

FIGURE 11.1 ■ Third Level Domains

When searching for a reliable hosting company, important factors to consider are customer service, knowledge of the industry, and business longevity in delivering Web technology solutions to real estate professionals.

DEVELOP A PLAN TO DRIVE PEOPLE TO YOUR SITE

Here are two simple ideas to drive traffic to your Web site.

1. Self Promotion. Consumers must know that you have a Web site—and the most effective way for them to find out is for you to tell them. Include your Web site address (URL [Uniform Resource Locator]) on all of your marketing materials, in all your advertisements, and in the signature of your e-mail, and include links to your site in specific e-mails that you push to your data base.
2. Use of Third Level Domains for your sign riders. Prior to the sale of a listing, instead of using a generic sign rider that states "Offered on the Internet," use inexpensive customized sign riders that state: "For More Information: *www.123RiverStreet.Your-Domain.com*"

When people drive by your listing, if they have an interest in the property, they may go to the site you name on the rider, which is just a page on your Web site offering information on that property and perhaps comparable properties. Instead of generic "Sold" riders, use customized SOLD riders such as *www.SOLD.YourDomain.com.*

FIGURE 11.2 ■ Viewing a Web Site with Different Browsers

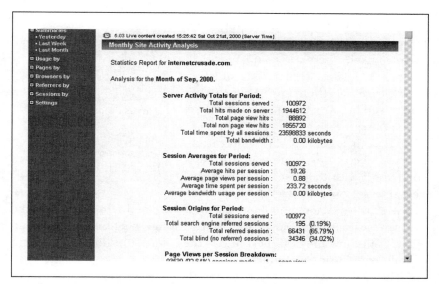

Screen shot reprinted by permission from Microsoft Corporation.

When potential buyers drive by your listing, they may be curious as to the sale price and may go to your Web site for information on the SOLD listing. You may also display comparable listing information at this URL. Neighbors who would never call you to ask what a property in their neighborhood sold for may go to your Web site for information on that sold listing. Everyone wants to know the selling price of their neighbor's house.

For more information on domains and Third Level Domains go to *http://Domains.RealTown.com* (notice that this is a Third Level Domain).

Remember, a Web site is a billboard in the middle of nowhere. Getting the most from your investment in a Web site will require constant effort on your part to monitor and measure results, making changes as needed.

USING SITE MANAGEMENT SOFTWARE

It is important to know how many people are visiting your Web site and how long they are remaining on the site, and even what browser and version they are using to view your site. Site management software is usually available through your Web host.

■ DEVELOPING LEADS FROM THE INTERNET

What about leads from the Internet? If you don't have the means to generate them yourself, there are companies that will help you with Internet leads for a fee. Weigh carefully their business proposition to you because they just might make economic sense.

There is a cost to lead generation and you need to examine your cost and compare it with the cost of some of the new referral programs available online.

> ■ **TIP**
> Take a look at your Web site in different browsers and different versions of browsers ... not all consumers use the same browser or version so it is a good idea to see how your site looks to others using different applications.

Those who are serious about being competitive in this business over the next five years must do some Web surfing to see what they might be up against and how they can best utilize the Internet in the development of their own business model.

The real estate sales business has always been about leads, one of the biggest time consumers in a real estate professional's day. Prospecting, working on the development of leads from cold calls to door hangers to direct mail, to signs on listings to classified ads are all designed to make the phone ring.

In the development of your business, where will the leads come from? How will they be matched and distributed in the age of the Internet? Is there is a more cost-effective way to develop leads than

> ■ **TIP**
> Create a survey for your Internet lead.

the old ways to which many agents and brokers have become accustomed? Make sure you take the time to explore and understand the online lead generation companies.

http://LeadGeneration.RealTown.com

To make your site a more effective tool, find out what works and what doesn't work from your customers and clients by asking them the following questions and others you create as you continue to define your Web presence:

1. How did you find my Web site?
2. Did it load quickly?
3. At what speed are you connected to the Internet?
4. What features of the site did you find most useful?
5. Did anything about the site annoy you?

Just asking questions shows you are interested in making the home-buying process better for your clients and customers. Many will not only give you feedback, but also be appreciative that you asked, because most real estate professionals do not ask. Just asking differentiates you from your competition.

Chapter Links:
http://InternetExplorer.RealTown.com
http://HomeGain.RealTown.com
http://HouseValues.RealTown.com
http://LendingTree.RealTown.com
http://Domains.RealTown.com
http://LeadGeneration.RealTown.com

■ REVIEW QUESTIONS

1. What is the generic name for the software used to surf the WWW and what is the most used product for this purpose?

   Answer: Browser/Microsoft Internet Explorer

2. (T/F) All you need to do is purchase a Web site from the first company that promises you that you will rank in the top ten of the major search engines and you will begin to receive more Internet leads than you can handle.

   Answer: False.

   Web sites are billboards in the middle of nowhere and this must be an ever-present consideration as you contemplate the purchase of a Web site. Since the commercialization of the browser in 1994, real estate professionals have wasted hundreds of millions of dollars on Web sites nobody visits.

3. Name two methods of driving traffic to your Web site.

   Answer: Placing your Web site address on all promotional materials

   Using third level domains on signs and in all written materials to drive traffic to specific content on your Web site

Chapter Twelve

Web Site Solutions for Real Estate Professionals

Losers fix the blame; winners fix what caused the problem.
DENIS WAITLEY
http://Motivation.RealTown.com

As you prepare to spend part of your marketing budget on a Web site, you must consider what you want your site to do or say. How does your Web site fit into your overall marketing plan? What is the primary objective of your site? If you think of your Web site as an advertisement or online personal brochure, then you should only expect people to drop by once, maybe a few times more if they need to contact you or forgot your phone number and happened to remember your domain name.

If, on the other hand, your Web site's purpose is to provide information to clients and prospects as an ongoing service, and you are diligent about updating the site's content—especially local content—you will likely get return visitors. What you want to establish online is no different than what you want to establish offline—relationships.

Create a Web site that people will visit and return to, even if they are not interested in buying and selling real estate. People buy and sell homes on average every five to eight years. Your objective is to get people to go to your site as often as possible, so when they are in the market for real estate services, they think of you.

■ TEMPLATE SITES WITH LIMITED CONTROL OVER CONTENT

National listing aggregators such as *REALTOR.com* offer real estate professionals the ability to be featured with their listings in a separate promotional site. The price for this type of Web site ranges from $300 to $1,000 and more annually (which typically includes one-time setup fees and first-year hosting fees), depending on the options you choose. Be aware that fees and services vary. Most listings in the country are represented on *REALTOR.com*.

> ■ **TIP**
> If your listings are on REALTOR.com because of marketing agreements with other international sites, your listing may appear on those sites as well. Be sure to know where your listings are displayed on the Internet and include that information in your listing presentations.

Template Web sites are typically not Web sites you own, but ones you have the right to use so long as you pay your annual renewal fee; annual fees vary. *REALTOR.com* sites have the objective of generating leads for the REALTOR® who has purchased the product (Web site). Be sure to ask other real estate professionals who have purchased Web sites from any of the aggregators before you spend your money. Don't let anyone "sell" you at a seminar. Do your own due diligence before purchasing. Don't be an impulse buyer of a Web site; do your planning and investigating first.

There are many companies offering Web sites and Web solutions to real estate professionals. One of the best ways to obtain recommendations and information on any Web provider you are thinking about doing business with is to ask about it on real estate industry specific listservs. RealTalk is an example of such a listserv (*http://RealTalk.RealTown.com*). The members of these online communities will surely have a great deal to say about their current (and sometimes their previous) Web providers.

If you intend to go the template site route, it is recommended that you make certain the site meets your objectives and is backed by a reputable company. There is much to be lost in terms of time and money when you select the wrong provider or site developer.

MASS CUSTOMIZATION SOLUTIONS

Real estate professionals are being bombarded with invitations to attend Web site seminars. Do not purchase a Web site at a Web site seminar unless you have done your homework first!!!

Homework includes visiting the sample sites being offered by the seminar companies and talking with other real estate professionals in your area who are also using the products you are examining. A key area of concern is the level of customer service that the product manufacturer and/or seminar company provides.

Most real estate professionals do not have an unlimited marketing budget. Make sure that your Web site choice is the proper solution for your real estate business.

Companies such as *Advancedaccess.com, Point2Agent.com, Homes.com,* and *REALTOR.com* offer mass customized solutions. When you examine their solutions consider cost, terms of renewal, content, ability to customize, and links to listings.

■ WEB-BASED EDITING APPLICATIONS

Today, some Web sites can be created, and maintained through the use of Web-based editing applications. This type of Web site can be edited from anyone's computer and can be done by a Web novice with little-to-no Web skills or programming skills. Editing allows for what some are referring to as **Web-on-the-fly.** Changes can be made instantly without waiting for a programmer and without paying programmer fees. Many real estate professionals today are taking advantage of this technology. Even if you have no desire to make the changes to your Web site yourself, you can assign them to an assistant who responds promptly and is paid much less than a programmer. Your Web site should be designed so it can be viewed in many browsers like Internet Explorer, AOL, and **Netscape,** and at different **resolutions.** Be sure to ask what the hosting company suggests to use for browsers and resolutions for best viewing your site.

Companies charge a fee for an annual hosting service that offers predesigned or semitemplated sites with **Web editing** functionality. There will be predetermined layouts that include specific placeholders for certain types of information. For example, each site will have your biography, header information, area information, links, listings, weather, education resources, news, etc. You will be provided with an administrative area (password protected) to fill in forms that will ulti-mately become the data on your site.

On an ongoing basis, you or your assistant will be able to go to the editing page at any time and simply paste in new text to update the site information. This can be cost-effective and can often result in a fairly powerful Web presence!

HTML GENERATORS

Another form of self-building Web site is known as an HTML gen-erator. It has several distinguishing features from the Web-on-the-fly model just discussed.

An HTML generator gives you a faster load time. It rebuilds your page only when you change it. The on-the-fly version takes even more time during busy parts of the day, as the **server** that is hosting it is not only building your page but everyone else's pages who are hosted on that server each time a browser requests it. It is also slower because the server your site is hosted on needs to contact the **database** multiple times to generate your page.

Imagine if you were calling an association that had a brand new receptionist. For every question you asked the receptionist, she'd have to ask someone else and then relay that answer to you. On the other hand, if the receptionist had been working there for a while and already knew how things worked, she'd be able to answer you instantly. Con-sider the on-the-fly pages the new receptionist and the HTML-gener-ated pages the experienced one.

The on-the-fly page requires at least three functions to be opera-tional, almost always on at least two different computers. The database must be running, the scripting engine (and any compiled components that it uses) must be running, and the Web server must be running. Each individual part of that triad has the potential to encounter a prob-lem and stop responding. The HTML-generated page is more reliable as it relies only on the Web server's functioning to serve content to the browser. Even if the database encounters an error that temporarily pre-vents you from making changes, the customer will see your site.

The on-the-fly page is created each time it is called. Because of this, you are stuck with the limitations of the system that generates it. Once the HTML generator has done its work, it has produced HTML files that you can then tweak yourself if you so desire. Do you want to add another picture to your home page? Move your pictures to different locations? Change the appearance of the buttons outside the scope your on-the-fly page allows? Maybe add a Flash insert? What about removing a default section of the generated page that you do not use? These things are difficult to impossible to do with an on-the-fly page. With an HTML-generated page, they are far easier. If you make a mistake, you can always regenerate the page and try again.

Because Web-on-the-fly ASP pages change content so frequently, many search engines treat them differently. They expect the content to be able to change at a moment's notice. When a search engine sees an HTML page, it expects the content to be more static. It is far more likely that your page will be full-text-indexed, for instance, so someone can search on any word on your page rather than just your meta-keywords, if the page name ends in .htm or .html.

http://InternetMarketingKit.RealTown.com

■ BUILD YOUR OWN WEB SITE

You can design, create, and maintain your Web site yourself only if you have the time, the desire, and the skills to do so. Even those who have opted to use some of the newer site design tools (FrontPage, DreamWeaver, etc.) will testify that building your own Web site takes more than a little technical skill. It is no small task to design and build a site that flows well and has the right mix of speed and functionality.

If, after careful consideration, you still want to go down the road of a self-developed Web site, then look into the tools that you will use to make it happen. Select the one that works for you and your skill level. If you are a technology wizard who writes base-level HTML and **cgi** code in your spare time, then you are all set. If, on the other hand, you are not at that level, we recommend that you try out the top two or three site development software packages: Microsoft FrontPage, Macro-media DreamWeaver, or Homesite. These tools will help you in many ways to design a site visually (drag and drop) and to automate the update process. The right tools will help you create the site without writing any code and use design templates to speed development and enhance look and feel.

You will still need to find and/or develop content. Remember, content is king. You need to target the audience and produce a site that meets their needs. You must still determine content access rights if using someone else's content. These software tools can help you to do all of this without becoming a programmer.

You will also need Web hosting and access to your site. The amount of space required will depend upon the complexity and functionality of your Web site.

CUSTOM WEB SITE (DESIGNER)

If you decide to control the information, design, and maintenance of your Web site but don't have the time, skills, or inclination to be the programmer, Webmaster, and content editor, then consider hiring a reputable firm to perform these functions. There are hundreds of Web designers ready to do your bidding—for a price. Many are able to do competent work even though they may be physically located in another part of the country. You must, by the way, perform the right amount of due diligence to determine that the firm you select will be able to perform to your expectations, and for a reasonable price. Be sure the Web designer understands your clearly stated expectations.

What is the best way to find a Web designer and Webmaster? Ask people who have used them. How do you find people who have used them? Look at the bottom of every Web site that catches your eye. There will usually be some link to the designer. As an example, it might say, "Site designed and hosted by . . ." This is their advertising. Use it to your advantage. Contact the Web site owner and get their opinion of the quality, responsiveness, and price of that Web designer or Webmaster. The site owner will be happy to complain if not satisfied. Likewise, the owner will be happy to brag if satisfied with the Webmaster's work.

Another way to check up on Web designers is to ask on listserv discussion groups such as RealTalk. Ask for references. There is no substitute for your own due diligence.

http://WebSiteSolutions.RealTown.com

■ LINKING, FRAMING, AND OPENING IN A NEW WINDOW

You do not have to create all of the content for your Web site. The Web is the great online library of the world. All you need to do is find content that fits the needs of your Web site's audience and you can link to it. The problem with linking is that you are sending contacts away from your site. Once you have accomplished the hard work of getting visitors to your site, you don't want to send them away.

A useful technique that will help you keep the visitor on your site is **framing.** Instead of linking away from your site, frame content into your site. Framing has another effect. If the visitor likes the framed content on your site and decides to bookmark it as a favorite, the title of the favorite will be your Web site's URL, not the framed site's URL.

When framing others' content, you must make sure that you do not violate copyright law or the framing policies of the company whose site you are framing. Web sites that do not wish to be framed can implement technology referred to as frame busters, which refreshes the framed Web site in a new browser on the viewer's monitor.

In framing, the site that wishes to borrow content will make a space for that content to appear within the confines of the framing Web site. In other words, you create a Web page that is made up of two or more boxes called frames. You then program one frame (box) to present a portion of your site information (buttons, links, headers, logos, etc.). You program the other frame (box) to go out and get another page of information and bring it into the second box so it is viewed in the context of the first box. Often, framing is used for site consistency and navigation purposes. Usually, framing is a legitimate procedure and can be a very effective design tool.

As a general policy, it is permissible to link or frame to any site you choose. Use common sense when framing. If you think the site owner would object (a competitor, for example) then do not frame. If you are notified by the site(s) to which you link or frame that this is considered a copyright violation, immediately take down the link or frame.

If you believe the information is valuable to your audience but don't like the frames that split your site, then have it open from your site in a new browser window. This creates a new stand-alone window containing the site with the information you want to make available to your visitors, while your site stays available in the original window. You have thus taken steps to avoid a copyright issue.

When you frame in someone else's content, they can change it without your knowledge. You could believe you are framing in an article extolling the schools in your region, then the provider could update the content to give a lesser or even negative review of the schools at a later time. While a link could suffer the same fate, it does not look as if you are providing bad content, as it does if you frame in their content.

Generally, you may link to any site you choose without first obtaining consent. The basic concept, philosophy, and technology of the Web argue in favor of linking. Likewise, it may be difficult to stop someone from linking to your site. In your business, you want all the traffic to your Web site you can get. If someone puts a link to your site on their site, "Thank You Very Much" is more than likely the appropriate thought.

To avoid any question of copyright infringement, you might want to obtain the site owner's permission to frame. Avoid deep linking several places within the site; instead, link or frame to the home page. Give attribution and credit to the site owner; avoid advertisements around the framed content. Use common sense when linking and framing.

> **TIP**
> In viewing a Web site framed within the main site, you might decide to find the URL of the framed site. If you go to bookmark the site to your Favorites, you will see that the URL displayed is that of the main site. Point your cursor to the framed pages you want, right click the mouse, and click on Properties. You can then copy the URL noted and paste it into the location bar of your browser, open that site, and then enter it into your Favorites folder.

■ WEB SITE CONTENT

Information is the currency of the 21st century. Today's new real estate professional has an opportunity to deliver valuable local information to a targeted audience.

Think of your Web site as a publishing vehicle and use your Web site to post valuable content. Information is content and content is why people will visit your Web site. Real estate professionals should build a Web site that people will visit and return to even when they are not interested in buying or selling real estate. In addition, your site should include real estate-specific information needed by customers and clients during the real estate sales cycle.

Another type of content is community created content. Having a Web publishing tool that allows your clients and prospects to publish information onto the Web specific to the community can generate traffic to your site. You might provide an area for "For Sale By Owners" to publish information about

> **TIP**
> Use a Web publishing tool and encourage members of the community to publish pictures and information on your Web site.

their homes. In doing so, they will send prospective buyers to your Web site. You can also encourage families to publish pictures of the children with their holiday gifts and they will then drive family members to your site to view the pictures. For more information on Web publishing tools go to:

http://CommunityBoard.RealTown.com

PERSONAL INFORMATION

Provide information about yourself, your company, and your services. Here is a comment from RealTalk, the number one online real estate community, about the benefit of providing good biographical data on your Web site:

"We have had two sales in the last six months totaling over $550,000 in sales and both clients said that the personal information on the Web site made them feel more comfortable with who we were and in turn became one of the deciding factors. The other thing we have done is been able to integrate mailers and newsletters to our sphere of influence that refer back to the personal sections of the Web site—generating traffic to the Web site and reminding people of what we do. Works great for us!!"

CURRENT INVENTORY OF PROPERTY
FOR SALE AS CONTENT

If you are a listing broker or associate, you will want your listings to be highlighted on your site. The easiest way to include your listings on your site, and perhaps many of the listings of other brokers in your area, is to find out what Internet Data Exchange (IDX) or Virtual Office Website (VOW) options are available through your MLS.

Under an NAR mandate, Multiple Listing Services are implementing reciprocity arrangements between themselves, local brokers, and third party vendors. Determine the IDX/VOW options available to you.

IDX solutions are available for most multiple listing services; the best source of information on possible IDX solution providers is through the MLS. IDX is considered advertising.

VOW solutions will be more expensive than IDX solutions in most markets. A VOW display of listing information is considered dissemination of information and there is a separate MLS policy and guidelines for VOWs.

http://IDXandVOW.RealTown.com

Assuming your listings are represented on one or more of the major aggregator sites, you will want to know how your listings are being displayed and represented on those sites. Many real estate professionals have never seen their listings on the Internet. You need to know what the national aggregators are saying about your listings so that you can respond to the issues if buyers or sellers have questions. Perhaps a new task on your listing checklist is to go to *REALTOR.com* and any other site where your listings appear and make sure they appear correctly and with accurate information. You might find it useful to make copies and e-mail them, snail mail them, or deliver them to the seller for review.

You should also include as content the listings of your company or listings from your national franchise. Consider bringing the entire inventory of *REALTOR.com* into your Web site, subject to *REALTOR.com's* framing policy.

PICTURES OF YOUR LISTINGS (AND VIRTUAL TOURS)

Various studies have shown that consumers like pictures. Listings with more pictures displayed on the Internet have a great chance of being requested for showings by buyers. Most MLSs today provide the opportunity for multiple photos and yet if you take a look at the listings in your MLS, you will find that most MLS subscribers use one, maybe two photos. If your MLS allows ten photos, use ten photos, and this will differentiate you from your competition.

If you are a buyer broker, having a property listing inventory to display on your Web site is a big plus. Also include articles about the benefits of working with a buyer broker, an explanation of agency, and issues that you believe add value to the services you bring to the consumer.

http://VirtualTours.RealTown.com

FREQUENTLY ASKED QUESTIONS AS CONTENT

During your career, you have probably developed a list of Frequently Asked Questions (FAQs) about real estate and the sales process. These FAQs can save you time and are a convenience for consumers. This is excellent content that you can send to clients when they request them (via an auto responder). You can also post these FAQs on your site.

Any question from clients that you have answered more than once is a candidate for your list of FAQs. Whether you are new to the business or a veteran, real estate professionals who are members of Real-Talk and other real estate listservs will be more than happy to share their list of FAQs with you—just ask.

Often FAQs can be the first place visitors look when they want to cut to the chase and go directly to the information they want. Visitors usually don't have a tolerance for wading through tons of otherwise useful information just to get a simple question answered. Consider making the FAQ list a valuable resource and timesaving device for your visitors. Use the online resources at your disposal through the real estate community to constantly add to your list.

LOCAL INFORMATION

When adding local information to your Web site, ask yourself what kinds of local information would be of interest. Here are some suggestions:

- School reports
- Shopping information and resources
- Park and recreational information
- Entertainment
- Employment data
- Comprehensive employer lists
- Transportation information
- High school athletic schedules, Little League schedules, scout troop schedules, church events, garage sales, etc.
- Holiday pictures of the neighbors, such as Halloween pictures of trick-or-treaters posted to your Web site. This type of content will drive the parents and grandparents to your site.
- Neighborhood descriptions and pictures
- A visual neighborhood tour and area information

- If the property is a common interest subdivision, CC & Rs, articles of incorporation, bylaws, pool rules, tenant rules, etc.
- Restaurants
- Auto repair
- Pool maintenance companies and other local vendors
- Lifestyles information (quality of life, cost of living)

You can publish this content on your Web site or it can be published on your Web site directly by the people who live in your marketing area with a community Web-publishing tool.

Neighborhood information makes for good content. There are software products available that facilitate the preparation and dissemination of reports covering neighborhood demographic, employment, school, and housing information. These reports often make an effective closing tool for listing appointments. One such software is *eNeighborhoods.com*.

NATIONAL INFORMATION

Here are some suggestions for national information:

- Travel and weather. By linking and framing other Web sites, you make it easy for your clients to access information they consider valuable to them—not everyone knows how to surf the Web.
- Kelly Blue Book
- Technology information
- Stock quotes
- Government agencies, such as the IRS

OTHER CONTENT

Here are some suggestions for additional content:

- Buyer's Book, which walks the consumer through the purchase process. This step-by-step approach also leads to the actual listing search.
- Maps and demographic data
- Web links and cyber tips
- State data
- Tax rates

- Real estate reports and third-party newsletters
- Homebuyer information center
- Articles
- Calculators
- Real Estate Glossary (a free glossary for your use is provided at *http://RealEstateGlossary.RealTown.com*)
- Real Estate Principles for Buyers and Sellers *(http://RealEstate-Principles.RealTown.com)*
- Contracts and Clauses *(http://Contracts.RealTown.com)*

Your Web site should make it easy for consumers to contact you by including one or more e-mail response forms on each page of the site. The site should also include your license information, brokerage name, and phone and fax numbers.

■ ENCOURAGING VISITORS TO RETURN TO YOUR WEB SITE

Determining ways to get visitors to your Web site is an important topic. Search engines, reciprocal cross-links, discussion groups, business cards, *REALTOR.com,* other marketing materials, and direct mail pieces showcasing some particular aspect of your site are helpful in driving traffic to your site.

Consider placing local content such as the Little League schedule or the movie schedules on your site. A direct mail piece to your database notifying them of content on your site may begin to drive traffic to your site. Web surfers first have to find your site and believe that it has valuable content; then they will keep coming back—and not just when they are in the market to buy or sell a house. If you have content which is available yet difficult to find otherwise, and that is appealing to your audience (it's all over the Internet), then let them know you have it by every means available, digital or otherwise.

Remember that people only buy a home every five to eight years. You want them visiting your Web site more often than that. Put content on your site that people will visit and return to even when they are not interested in buying and selling real estate. Use your conventional means of disseminating information, your conventional marketing plan (advertising and direct mail) to drive people to your Web site. More traffic will result in more sales and referrals. Contacts create contracts—contact with people creates opportunity. That has always been the case and it is no different on the Internet.

■ WEB SITE TIPS

Here are some general suggestions and cautions:

- Don't let your unavailable listings (Sold/Expired/Off Market) remain on the site; disciplinary action could result for unauthorized advertising.
- Don't strip headers from your Web site visitors' information for e-mail addresses without disclosure. Learn more about **permission marketing.**
- Don't expect search engines to bring you much traffic unless you are willing to commit resources (time and/or capital)—and even then, you may not see significant results.
- Don't violate copyright laws—respect the property compilations from other broker sites, including the MLS database.
- Don't violate state licensing law regarding disclosure and advertising.
- Your Web site is your Internet face to the world. Avoid poor grammar and misspelled words.
- Check the sites you link to (or frame) periodically to make sure you have no broken links (links that no longer exist) or missing graphics.
- Make sure your contact information is up-to-date and accurate.
- Avoid large graphics. Your typical Web surfer will become impatient and leave your site after several seconds of waiting for images to download. Consider inserting small thumbnail photos that, when clicked, appear in larger formats.
- Think about your audience: Who are they, why are they there, and what do they expect to find? Make the site easy for them to navigate. Most people are still pretty new to the Internet.
- Your Web site should make it easy for consumers to contact you via an e-mail response form. Respond promptly.
- The site should also include your real estate license information and name of broker and company if required by state licensing law.

Your site is like an interactive electronic information resource. This resource is a good way to gather leads and feedback in an efficient and cost-effective manner, as well as showcase your company's strength and technological sophistication. Use free reports to help gather the names of the visitors to your site. You can offer to e-mail information to a visitor, information such as how to negotiate the purchase of a home and how to stage your home for showing. The technology that allows you to do this is an auto-reply (auto-responder) built into your site. Visitors simply enter their e-mail addresses into a field on your site and the report is automatically sent to them. You then receive their e-mail addresses for follow-up.

Chapter Links:
http://RealTalk.RealTown.com
http://WebSiteSolutions.RealTown.com
http://InternetMarketingKit.RealTown.com
http://CommunityBoard.RealTown.com
http://IDXandVOW.RealTown.com
http://VirtualTours.RealTown.com
http://RealEstateGlossary.RealTown.com
http://RealEstatePrinciples.RealTown.com
http://Contracts.RealTown.com

■ REVIEW QUESTIONS

1. People buy and sell real estate how often on average?

   Answer: Every five to eight years

2. (T/F) Web sites should be more than resume pages and have more than just generic information—they should not be like everyone else's Web site.

   Answer: True.

   Think of your Web site as a publishing vehicle and use your Web site to post valuable content. Information is content and content is why people will visit your Web site. Real estate professionals should build a Web site that people will visit and return to even when they are not interested in buying or selling real estate.

3. (T/F) Use multiple images to display your listings on your Web site and elsewhere on the Internet.

   Answer: True.

   Various studies have shown that consumers like pictures. Listings with more pictures displayed on the Internet have a great chance

of being requested for showings by buyers. Most MLSs today provide the opportunity for multiple photos; yet, if you take a look
at the listings in your MLS, you will find that most MLS subscribers use one, maybe two photos. If your MLS allows ten photos,
use ten photos and this will differentiate you from your competition.

Chapter Thirteen

Eight Suggestions for Your Internet Marketing Strategy

Expect the best, plan for the worst, and prepare to be surprised.
DENIS WAITLEY
http://Motivation.RealTown.com

Complete Internet marketing strategy consists of two major components, an **e-mail presence** and a Web presence. For maximum results, your Internet marketing strategy must be integrated into your overall marketing strategy whenever possible.

Creating an Internet presence that will bring you visible and tangible results—more money in your pocket, more efficient use of your time, an increase in the number of buyers and sellers you can work with at a time—requires a commitment to accomplishing a series of projects or tasks. This list can appear so daunting that it scares many people from taking the first step.

The following list of suggestions for developing your Internet marketing strategy is not an all-or-nothing proposition. As was the case with the e-mail marketing strategy discussed earlier, you do not have to implement all of the suggestions to receive tangible benefits from the suggestions you do implement. The benefits will multiply as you integrate more of the suggestions. The key is your commitment to success. *It's the little things that make a difference.*

Don't worry about being perfect—the most important thing is to begin.

■ 1. ACQUIRE YOUR OWN DOMAIN

The foundation of both your e-mail presence and your Web presence is ownership and control of your domain. As a real estate professional, you are likely to be an independent contractor. Your career relies on brand marketing and making your brand as well known in your market area as you possibly can.

Most of your new and repeat business is a direct result of your efforts and reputation. You have created your brand in the marketplace, based on either your name or the name of your team. You go out of your way to make your name known, to brand yourself in the community as the real estate professional of choice, using all the conventional methods of marketing and advertising at your disposal. Examples are business cards; brochures; giveaways (pads, pens, flyswatters, magnets, rain caps, letter openers); signs; riders; bus stop benches; billboards; and magazines.

The presence you have created in the business (which has been built over time and has a cumulative effect) can now be transitioned to the Internet and multiplied dramatically. You can take advantage of all of your offline branding efforts and expand them to the Web by using your brand name as your domain name. If you are known as Bill Smith offline, you want to be known as *BillSmith.com* online. If you are known as the Bill Smith Team offline, you want to be known as *BillSmithTeam.com* online.

Owning your own domain is the first essential element of a successful and continuous Internet marketing strategy. It gives you the ability to maintain both a permanent e-mail address and a **permanent Web site address.** The money you spend to promote and build both your name and domain will have a cumulative effect over time, as one enhances the other, just as your current conventional marketing plan has done in the past. You are now looking to the future.

Reserving the domain name of your special brand is becoming more difficult, as others have already taken so many domains. Determine if your brand name is still available. If it is, count yourself among

> ## ■ TIP
> Reserve, at a minimum, your name, if it is available. While it is true that many real estate professionals are thinking about the salability of their business in the future, many successful businesses were built around a name, which has the advantage of already being known by your past clients. Examples are names such as Sears, J.C. Penney, Arthur Young, Ford, Dean Witter, Long and Foster, Weichert, and many others. Your name is your brand and your brand is your name.

the lucky and reserve it immediately—for multiple years. If it is not, be creative and chose an online brand that will take advantage of the name you have built offline (use your middle initial, or a hyphen, or add a word such as team, group, or the name of your city or geographic location).

■ 2. MAKE THE MOST OF YOUR CURRENT INTERNET PRESENCE

Where are your listings currently appearing on the Internet? On *REALTOR.com?* Listings on *REALTOR.com* appear on other national Web sites. Perhaps they are on *Yahoo.com,* your local MLS, or a franchise site. Understand how and where your listings and services are currently being marketed on the Internet and then decide what you can do to improve your current position. Are you maximizing your current exposure?

Are photos appearing with your listings? Many consumers have stated that they usually skip over the pictureless listings and go directly to the ones with pictures. This is just one important reason to own a digital camera. Make it a tool you take to every listing appointment and submit the maximum number of pictures allowed to Web sites where your listings will appear.

Are you using **virtual tour technology?** Take your own virtual tour, too, if your camera has the capability. In the next few years, it is quite likely that all sellers will require the listing broker to include virtual tour technology as an essential part of their Internet marketing efforts.

http://VirtualTours.RealTown.com

■ 3. REVIEW YOUR CURRENT OFFLINE MARKETING STRATEGY

Developing your Internet marketing strategy requires that you first review your offline marketing efforts and strategies.

Are the following some of the methods you are now using to market your listings and services offline?

- Telling everyone you know that you are in the real estate business
- Making your business cards available to anyone who will take one

- Writing letters and postcards and conducting direct mail campaigns to past clients, spheres of influence, and geographic "farms"
- Collecting written testimonials and making them available to prospects
- Giving away promotional materials such as calendars, magnets, pads, and flyswatters with your name, phone, and fax number on them
- Cold calling
- Branding yourself at every opportunity, in the eyes of the public and in your spheres of influence

Chances are that you employ all of the above techniques with the intention of getting appointments to make listing presentations or to get buyer-showing opportunities, either through direct contact or referral. Once you get the appointment, you more than likely will be making a presentation in competition with several other real estate professionals. If it is a listing appointment, your job is to win at the appointment—to prove to the sellers that you are different than other real estate professionals and that you are best equipped to sell the house for them in a reasonable period of time. Your listing presentation is designed to convince them of that fact.

At your listing presentation you present your marketing plan, which may consist of some or all of the following:

- Classified advertising in the local newspaper
- Flyers of individual listings, which are available at an open house and in sign boxes
- Brochures, usually for upscale properties
- Magazine advertising, usually for your more expensive listings
- Signs, still one of the most effective methods of marketing
- Sign riders, how to contact you, the listing agent
- Open house

Today, sellers are beginning to ask, "How will you market my home on the Internet?" Part of your listing presentation must show sellers your Internet marketing strategy, as well as your conventional marketing strategy.

■ 4. INTEGRATE YOUR CURRENT MARKETING EFFORTS WITH YOUR INTERNET EFFORTS

Creating a successful Internet marketing strategy requires the integration of proven, successful, conventional marketing strategies with the marketing opportunities available on the Internet.

Internet marketing is not stand-alone marketing. At this stage of the online revolution, any person or company completely abandoning successful marketing tools in favor of the Internet is destined to fail. The Internet gives you the opportunity to market yourself, your services, and your listings to a wider audience. Internet marketing is very similar to existing marketing processes. Like all advertising and marketing, Internet marketing requires consistency and repetition if you hope to realize maximum reward for your efforts.

Think of the Internet as a marketplace where people go and where you present information about products and services. Ask yourself how you can utilize your current marketing methods (at which you are already so good) to tell people about your Web site.

Your Web site is your place on the Internet. While search engines may help drive people to your Web site, it will be your individual marketing efforts that bring the fastest and best results. The first step, simple and yet neglected by so many real estate professionals, is putting your Web site address (URL) on all your conventional marketing pieces. Your URL should be your domain, a permanent URL that you brand by displaying it everywhere.

Examples and recommendations for publicizing your URL include the following:

- **Voicemail**—"For additional information please visit me online at *www.MyBrand.com*"
- **Business Cards**—"e-mail: Me@MyBrand.com, Web site: *http://www.MyBrand.com*"
- **E-mail**—Include your e-mail address and Web site address in the signature of every message and reply
- **Advertising**—include your e-mail address and Web site address in every ad, including classified ads; include your e-mail address and Web site address on your car license frame, magnetic signs, open house signs, and for sale signs
- **Online Community**—Participate and promote yourself via your e-mail signature

- **Newsletters, Farming Promotional, and Other Print Material**—Include your e-mail address and Web site address in every piece
- **Fax-back**—Include your e-mail address and Web site address on every one
- **Letterhead**—Include your e-mail address and Web site address
- **Signs and Sign Riders**—Include your Web site address and possibly **Third Level Domains** such as *Sold.YourBrand.com* and *123RiverStreet.YourBrand.com*

■ 5. CREATE COPIES OF YOUR INTERNET MARKETING PRESENTATION

Your listing presentation and prelisting package should contain paper copies (**atoms**) of the following:

- Your personal Web site
- The traffic count of your Web site through the use of site management software, available through your domain host
- Your listings, which are already on the Internet (on *REALTOR.com,* for example)
- If your listings are on *REALTOR.com* or another other national Web site, include site statistics with the disclaimer: "The following information is for example purposes only and may not be current numbers."
- Total page views each month
- Average views received for each listing
- Total number of listings
- Your broker's site and site statistics
- Franchise site and your listings currently on the site
- Copy of auto responder content when auto responder is in classified ads
- The benefits of working with a new real estate professional

Remember, *it's the little things that make a difference.*

FIGURE 13.1 ■ Using "Print Screen" To Capture Web-Based Material

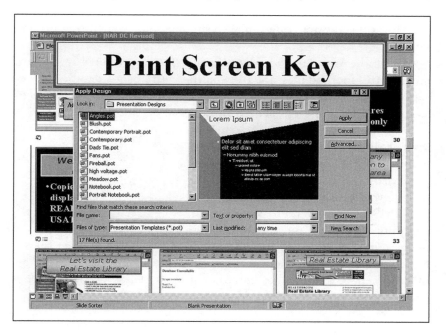

Screen shot reprinted by permission from Microsoft Corporation.

FIGURE 13.2 ■ Using "Alt+Print Screen" to Capture Web-Based Material

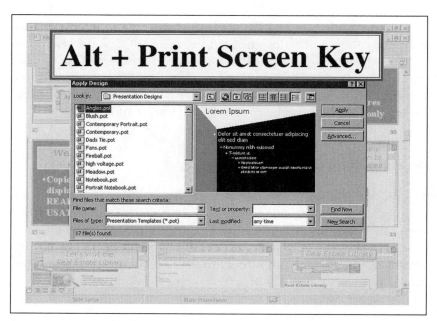

Screen shot reprinted by permission from Microsoft Corporation.

CAPTURE AND PRINT WEB-BASED INFORMATION

How do you print copies of Web site pages for your listing presentation?

Go to the Web site and select "Print." Because of the way sites are created, this method may not give you the entire page. Another way to capture a Web site (or anything being displayed on your desktop) is to use a technique known as **screen capture.**

Open presentation software such as Microsoft PowerPoint. Create several blank slides. Then, while online, open your browser and go to the Web site page(s) you want to make copies of. Tap the "PrtSc" (Print Screen) key on your computer keyboard and then paste the image onto a PowerPoint slide. Connect to a color printer, print and you are ahead of 99 percent of your competition when it comes to communicating Web marketing strategies to prospective sellers.

> ### ■ TIP
> For copying information right off your desktop, capturing Web sites for a presentation, etc., use:
>
> PrtSc—Captures entire screen
> Alt + PrtSc—Captures active window only
>
> The image is now on the clip board and can be pasted into an application such as PowerPoint or Word.

■ 6. CREATING A BUYER INTERNET RESOURCE PRESENTATION

If you have buyers who are not familiar with the availability of listing information on the Internet, tell them how to find the real estate sites. Also tell them how to search for property and how to contact you should they find a property they are interested in, would like more information about, or would like to see. You add value as a real estate professional by helping the consumer make sense of the Internet.

■ 7. RECIPROCAL LINKS

You can share the cost and maximize the exposure by entering into reciprocal linking with other Web site owners whose site might attract consumers who might become your prospects; for example, the local pest control operator, the interior designer, the moving company, the gardener, etc. Each of these could benefit by being linked from your Web site. You, likewise, will benefit by being a link on each of theirs!

FIGURE 13.3 ■ Third Level Domain

The best way to make this happen is to craft a reciprocal link program, including a letter (e-mail) to be used as an invitation to join the linking team. The message must answer two questions:

a. Will it cost me anything? Usually no
b. What will it do for me? Source of potential qualified leads

In a program such as this, you inform the potential partner of the type and location of the link you will provide for them, as well as the type and location you expect in return. Once you have an agreement, monitor the results and keep the partner up-to-date on any successful referrals you are able to track.

■ 8. THIRD LEVEL DOMAINS

The Registrant (Owner) of a Second Level Domain is in control of issuing Third Level Domains, provided the domain host is capable and willing to allow Third Level Domains.

Use of Third Level Domains can help you market the services and benefits you offer, as well as market yourself at the same time.

The most well-known Third Level Domain is WWW. A domain host can replace the WWW with any description or wording the holder of the Second Level Domain requests.

Examples:

http://Listings.YourBrand.com—This Third Level Domain could point to a page with current listings.
http://Sold.YourBrand.com—This Third Level Domain could point to a Web page of sold listings.
http://OpenHouse.YourBrand.com—This Third Level Domain could point to a page of open house schedules.

There are many Web marketing tools available to today's real estate professional to help you differentiate yourself from your competition; tools such as online newsletters, virtual tours, and others. Most of these tools can be used with any Web site, because they offer you a unique URL. Often that URL is so long that, when embedded in an e-mail message, it breaks the link, making the link ineffective. A way to prevent this, and brand your domain as well, is by using Third Level Domains to hide or mask that long URL.

Because signs remain one of the most effective marketing tools in the real estate professional's arsenal—consistently accounting for between 35 and 40 percent of all information that homebuyers get about a property, according to NAR surveys of buyers—sign riders that include your URL information are a terrific way to promote your Web site. However, if you want to differentiate yourself, you need to do more than just include "Offered on the Internet" on your yard signs. Think how much more compelling it would be to Internet-savvy customers if your sign read: "For more information, visit *http://123RiverStreet.YourDomain.com.*" What could be more appealing and easier than a Web page devoted just to the house they like?

You or your Web designer can put specific information about 123 River Street at that Web site location so prospects don't have to waste time searching your entire site for the particular house in which they have an interest. You might also want to consider adding links to comparable properties on each Third Level Domain page so that prospects won't just look and leave if they don't like what they see in the first property. And don't forget to include a link that will take visitors back to your main home page.

■ **TIP**

Make sure your domain host allows you to create all the Third Level Domains you want to create, and at no additional charge. Remember, there are three types of hosting—domain hosting, e-mail hosting, and Web site hosting.

You can accomplish this marketing coup by creating Third Level Domains and pointing them to the section (or file) on your Web site you dedicate for each of your listings. You can then buy inexpensive custom riders for your signs displaying that Web site address—*http:// 123RiverStreet.YourDomain.com*.

Your domain host should offer you the ability to inexpensively create Third Level Domains. For example:

http://123RiverStreet.YourDomain.com
http://FeaturedProperty.YourDomain.com
http://Sold.YourName.com
http://CondoProject.YourName.com

MASKING AND THIRD LEVEL DOMAINS

Masking is a technique whereby the Third Level Domain points to a Web file on an Internet server and the Third Level Domain is actually viewed in the browser of the Web surfer instead of the name of the file on the server upon which the file sits. Many Internet Web products today are actually files sitting on an Internet server having the address structure of the product provider, which can be confusing and not intuitive.

Examples:
http://iccb.internetcrusade.com/iccb/display/index.asp?BoardID=43

This is a unique URL (Uniform Resource Locator or Web site address) for an InternetCrusade Community Board. This URL would look better in an e-mail marketing piece as:

http://CommunityBoard.InternetCrusade.com
(and in the browser address bar of the Web surfer)

Clicking on the URL *http://CommunityBoard.InternetCrusade.com* would take the visitor to the URL *http://iccb.internetcrusade.com/iccb/ display/index.asp?BoardID=43*.

The browser would indicate the proper branded Third Level Domain in the address indicator of the browser (*http://Community Board.InternetCrusade.com*). This is masking.

Chapter Links:
http://VirtualTours.RealTown.com
http://ThirdLevelDomains.RealTown.com

■ REVIEW QUESTIONS

1. (T/F) Complete Internet marketing strategy consists of two major components, an e-mail presence and a Web presence.

   Answer: For maximum results, your Internet marketing strategy must be integrated into your overall marketing strategy whenever possible.

2. (T/F) While search engines may help to drive people to your Web site, it will be your individual marketing efforts that bring the fastest and best results.

   Answer: True.

   There are complex Web strategies and there are basic Web strategies. Don't leave out the inexpensive, easy strategies. The first step, simple and yet neglected by so many real estate professionals, is putting your Web site address (URL) on all your conventional marketing pieces. Your URL should be your domain, a permanent URL that you brand by displaying it everywhere.

3. (T/F) Your URL should be your domain, a permanent URL that you brand by displaying it everywhere. Name five examples.

   Answer: Voicemail—"For additional information please visit me online at *www.MyBrand.com*"

   Business Cards—e-mail: Me@MyBrand.com, Web site: *http:// www.MyBrand.com*

   E-mail—include your e-mail address and Web site address in the signature of every message and reply.

   Advertising—include your e-mail address and Web site address in every ad, including classified ads. Include your e-mail address and Web site address on your car license frame, magnetic signs, open house signs, for sale signs.

   Online Community—Participate and promote yourself via your e-mail signature.

   Newsletters, Farming Promotional, and Other Print Material—Include your e-mail address and Web site address in every piece.

Fax-back—Include your e-mail address and Web site address on every one.

Letterhead—Include your e-mail address and Web site address.

Signs and Sign Riders—Include your Web site address and possibly Third Level Domains such as *Sold.YourBrand.com* and *123RiverStreet.YourBrand.com*.

Chapter Fourteen

The Power of Virtual Communities
The Power of RealTalk

The primary success factor is knowing how to learn from others and rely on yourself.
DENIS WAITLEY
http://Motivation.RealTown.com

Major benefits from participation in online communities include referrals from other real estate professionals, leads for listings and sales, a resource for information at your fingertips, and collective power with vendors.

■ **INCREASING VALUE OF VIRTUAL COMMUNITIES**

As more and more people go online, and as the conversations online continue, more virtual communities are being formed. These communities become the foundation of marketing and customer service in an online world. Virtual communities give people with similar experiences and interests the opportunity to come together—freed from the restraints of time and space—to form beneficial relationships. An online community is a network of people sharing with one another.

> ■ **TIP**
> Join the RealTalk Online Community; go to http://RealTalk.RealTown.com and subscribe to either the RealTalk Digest or Immediate Mode. Digest is a periodic e-mail (one to two a day) with all the contributions consolidated. Immediate mode subscriptions will send you each member's contributions as they are released by the listserv moderator. Immediate mode could result in 100 or more individual e-mails a day—which is no big deal if you are an e-mail powerhouse.

157

The power of online communities expands exponentially as members join the community. It is the power of networking and can be described mathematically by Metcalfe's Law. Robert Metcalfe, the inventor of a networking technology known as Ethernet, first noticed this principle. Metcalfe's idea was based on a telephone network. One telephone and one user have very little value. Add a second telephone and a second user and you have increased the value of the individual units by creating a network of two telephones (two nodes). The total number of potential calls in a telephone network is the sum of all possible pairings of people with phones. When you add one new user, many new pairings are possible (the total of all the network users pairing with the new addition). In a network of 100, adding one new member increases the total number of pairings in that network by 100. Online networks, like personal networks in real life, provide opportunity for three-way, four-way, and many-way communications that enhance the power of the network even more. During the late 1970s, Metcalfe was promoting a combination of Ethernet, Unix, and TCP/IP (Internet protocol) as a way to make larger networks out of smaller ones. In 1980, he began to formulate what became known as Metcalfe's Law:

Value (of a network) equals N (nodes) squared

The more nodes there are in a network, the greater the value of the network.

Or, the more members there are in an online community, the greater the value of the online community.

The value of an online network (any network) increases as the membership increases. In other words, increasing the number of nodes (people, in the case of a virtual community) arithmetically will result in an exponential explosion in the value of the network—just adding a few members can dramatically increase the value of the network for all members.

■ COMMUNITY FORMATS

There are a number of different technology formats that allow the exchange of ideas and information as well as the development of an online community:

- Listservs, e-mail lists, which are very effective because most people visit their e-mail inbox multiple times a day.

- Bulletin boards, a place on the WWW where members go to post ideas and thoughts, contributions.
- Chat, which requires all participants to be online at the same time typically, to have a conversation.

COMMUNITY-CREATED CONTENT

A defining characteristic of maturing online (virtual) communities is community-created content. Members of virtual communities derive, over time, greater value from community-created content than from the more conventional forms of published content available at Web sites. The Listserv community known as RealTalk *(http://RealTalk.Real Town.com)* is the classic example of real estate community-created content. At times the content may bore some, but over time, there is always information of interest to large numbers of the community members. RealTalk utilizes Listserv technology discussed in a previous chapter. E-mail is quick and convenient, and the first place most people go when they go online is to check their e-mail.

Community-created content is typically produced in real time and relates to the experience of most of the members of the community.

Community generated content not only takes place online—there is often sharing and networking offered in private off-list discussions. Here are some examples to give you a flavor of various online conversations on RealTalk:

Example 1

USER 1 This evening I had an Excel file to an AOL client bounce back. Is this the same problem?

J.J.
Rockport, IL

USER 2 Matt replies: You might try creating a temporary Web page and sending a link rather than an attachment. If you need help doing this contact me offline.

USER 3 I could not find the beginning of this thread, but, FWIW, I have been sending Excel attachments to customers and clients weekly for six or seven years now and I have not had any problems. I sent an Excel attachment to an old AOL account this morning and it was received, downloaded, and opened just fine. I use Excel 4.0 (hey, it still seems to work) and Outlook Express on a Mac.

V.N.
Madison, WI

Example 2

In response to: How do you handle a buyer who is continuously late arriving at showings that are set up? I have tried to explain to them in a nice manner that I have other clients and usually have other appointments after theirs, but they continuously show up 20–30 minutes late to our appointments.

You need to start with the first appointment with a buyer. I usually tell buyers I cannot wait more than 15 minutes for them to arrive. If they are running late, please call me, and we can schedule another appointment. Over the years only a few have become upset. Hope this helps.

S.O.
Bridgeport, CT

Example 3

In RealTalk V1 #761 USER 1 "Marshall" wrote: Well, if you can't find a label that will fit, why not format and order a self inking rubber stamp from Office Depot for about $14 and change. You get a low cost alternative until you order your cards with printing on the reverse side in the future.

USER 2 Amen, Marshall! I've been really surprised at how many RealTalkers would take the time to paste labels on the backs of business cards. Gosh, business cards are not that expensive, but our time is.

But on the subject of business cards, I have an idea that has worked well for me in the past: have more than one kind of card.

When I went to my first national convention, I realized the card that I was using at home was less than effective as a tool for generating referrals. So I decided to design my cards according to the market I was going after. This is really only an extension of what I tell seller prospects: I market my listings to two groups. Buyers and REALTORS®.

My home card had, in addition to the required stuff, my smiling face and a nice little request for referrals—"The highest compliment I can receive . . ."—in blue italics with my first name below. Of course everyone knows it's not hand written (although next time, I may use the font of my handwriting I had made), but I was going for the "warm, fuzzies" here. What I don't include is my home phone number or cell number or any of the designations. This is for the public and they don't know what the alphabet soup means.

My REALTOR® referral card does not have my picture, but is printed on a picture postcard type background of the Statue of Liberty and lower Manhattan. I figure that only locals know that Jersey City, NJ, is right across the Hudson River from lower Manhattan. I'm looking for referrals from REALTORS® who are far more likely to have referrals to NYC than Jersey City. This card has my designations, because the target market for the cards knows what the initials mean. Although I always say, "I don't put my photo on the card because I want you to remember where I am, rather than what I look like," last year at the RE/MAX Convention a couple of people said, "Oh, I remember you from your card!" Go figure.

I actually have a third card—really cheap—which I use for key tags for my listings. I laminate the card using peel and stick luggage tag markers. A showing agent can peek at the back for square footage, taxes, etc., and my contact info is there in an emergency.

Lest you think I am a total spendthrift, old, obsolete, business cards travel with me to conventions. They are the ones I drop into vendor fishbowls for door prize drawings. And, if I ever use up all my old cards, I'll dip into my key tag cards for the fishbowls.

L.T.
Jersey City, NJ

Example 4

USER 1 Donna writes: I'm preparing a PowerPoint slide presentation for my Board of REALTORS®, showing enhancements and changes that we have made to our MLS system.

I only know enough about PP to do some basic slides. Do any of your savvy people out there know if an Adobe PDF file or an MS Publisher file can be converted to a PowerPoint slide? (The original was done in an MS Publisher file and has some graphics.)

USER 2 Hi Donna, a simple way to do this is to use the "Print Screen" feature. Whatever you want to put on a PowerPoint slide:

1. Bring it up on your "Desktop" and maximize it.
2. Hit the "Print Screen (Prnt Scrn)" key which is usually up in the right hand section of your keyboard.
3. Go to a blank PP slide and "Paste" (Control V/Edit-Paste/Right Click-Paste).
4. If the image does not fit the screen, size it by grabbing the image (click on the image, put the cursor on the images), and move the image to a corner of the slide. Then put the cursor on one of the corners and drag it to fill the slide.

If you have a photo to insert, go to a blank slide and:

1. Click on "Insert" at the top of your screen.
2. A Window will open and you can then locate the photo you want to insert and select and size as above.

I sometimes copy any photo I want to insert to my desktop so it is easy to locate :-)

S.K.
San Diego, CA

Example 5

Dave wrote: If it is a supra key box that is jammed, sliding your business card or something else that is thin like that may unjam it. Just a little trick I learned that saved me having to come back later.

You can also get a simple tool at any automotive store that is used to set the gas on spark plugs. We buy one for each agent to carry in their purse/pocket. Really saves the day in the cold Missouri winters when the batteries get weak and it won't 'spit' out the key holder. You can't break into the box, but if you get a click and it doesn't release, then it will 'help' it along.

G.J.
Biloxi, MS

COMMUNITIES AS USER GROUPS

The best and most useful working knowledge about new technology products comes out of user groups. Today on the Internet, at various locations, you can find user groups for just about any interest or avocation. RealTalk sometimes functions similarly to a user group, as the community members share experiences in areas ranging from software and hardware to marketing programs and Internet products.

http://BestOfRealTalk.RealTown.com

There is much written about the empowered and connected consumer and how real estate professionals must be ready to serve their needs. While this is absolutely true, let's not forget—and let's not let vendors of real estate products and services forget—that real estate professionals are also empowered and connected consumers to whom vendors must answer. Real estate professionals today have one major forum, RealTalk, for demanding value for their money when purchasing technology products and services, or any products and services from any vendor.

With online communities, people are connected to people. This is a powerful force because, "No one is as smart as everyone" (Larry Keeley). There is a world of online communities out there for you to discover, as your interest and time allow. If knowledge is power, then members of online communities have the power!

Participate in the RealTalk Listserv for the real estate industry. Consider this community a resource and your pipeline to the latest in the world of real estate, from technology tips to effective marketing strategies. Share ideas with the industry's best. Presidents of companies will hear your voice as they observe and, in some cases, participate in online conversations about their company, products, and services.

The RealTalk community helps real estate professionals take back their future. To join this free Listserv, send an e-mail to RealTalk@InternetCrusade.com, or go to *Realtalk.Realtown.com.*

POWER WITH VENDORS

Vendors are often members of industry-specific online communities or receive copies of the messages exchanged within the communities about their products and services. Often they elect to respond. In some cases, their response is an explanation to clear up a misunderstanding or miscommunication. At times, complaints are addressed and refuted. The vendor also has the opportunity to take immediate action to resolve the issue and report the resolution to the community members! Vendors who promptly address the needs and concerns of their customers gain by developing a product and brand loyalty from the community members.

To understand this, realize that there are literally thousands of current and potential users of a vendor's product who read and participate in these discussion lists. All have the potential to walk into an office meeting and report what they just read on RealTalk or some other Listserv discussion. Effectively, tens or even hundreds of thousands of real estate professionals might hear the "bad news about a product" and the vendor knows that! Any vendors with an eye toward the future know that they cannot ignore such a powerful user group.

INTERNET PROSPECTING THROUGH COMMUNITY

Contact with people creates opportunity—and the Internet creates a variety of ways to contact and connect with people. The Internet is the network of networks, and real estate is a networking business.

A large part of the job for any sales professional is prospecting and working a territory—be it geographical or a circle of friends and acquaintances, sometimes referred to as a sphere of influence. The Internet is a vast, relatively untouched territory, which can easily and effectively be reached on even a modest marketing budget. Information is a driving force for consumers today. The real estate professional who has the ability to gather, position, and distribute information in a cost-effective manner will be the big winner.

Prospecting is the process of gathering a database of suspects through advertising and marketing, then filtering that database into a list of prospects, which can further be filtered into a list of clients. These clients have the goal of purchasing or selling a home. Prospecting is one of the primary functions of a real estate sales professional. You have to keep your pipeline full. The new real estate professional must prospect both offline and online.

Methods currently used to develop leads in the real or conventional world include the following:

- For Sale signs
- Advertising listings in local newspaper to attract buyer calls
- Marketing for listings, including direct mail, brochures, magazines, give-aways
- Relationship building by joining and participating in the community through churches and Little League

- Professional Referral Networks Service organizations such as e-PRO, WCR, CRS, ABR

■ PROSPECTING WITH TECHNOLOGY

Skills you develop participating in online communities can come in handy when working to develop relationships with potential clients and customers online.

Let's call the process of getting and developing leads through Internet resources "cyber-prospecting." You can apply many of the same conventional processes to cyber-prospecting that you use in conventional prospecting.

Listings are inexpensively advertised on the Internet. If you have listings advertised on your Web site or another site such as *REALTOR.com,* interested buyers may e-mail you that they are interested in the property. Even if prospective buyers do not contact you directly, they may end up buying your listings through another real estate professional, having first viewed the property online.

Often, potential Internet buyers are in the early stages of the home buying process, searching for property listings far in advance of actually looking for homes through a real estate professional. Many search the Internet to check prices, read tutorials, and more. Your ability to provide them with information on the area and the availability of properties coupled with your skill at building an online relationship will result in a sale—in some cases six months to a year in the future.

HANDLING INTERNET LEADS

How do you handle Internet buyer leads? The same way you would handle in-person leads—provide information and service to the potential client. You will most likely use e-mail as the primary method of communication. Find out the client's bandwidth—you don't want to send large files if the client is connected at a slow speed. Provide relevant information, and return all e-mail in a timely manner. At the same time, check the client's message for a signature or vCard that might offer a telephone number. If it is not there, it is appropriate to ask for the client's number in a reply message, only if you are giving information that was requested. For example, you might say: "I am attaching the information—that you requested. As an added benefit to you, please send me your contact information: telephone, address, etc.—so that I can call you with additional details not listed in the flyer."

If you use Microsoft's Outlook, Outlook Express, or many of the other top-tier e-mail programs, you can usually right click (click the right mouse button once) to be able to add the person to your address book. To add the person using Outlook Express for example:

Right click on the sender's name or e-mail address and select "Add to Address Book."

You are offered a pop-up window with tabs for many different types of information (home, business, personal, etc.). The information in the header is already filled in. Add whatever additional information you can glean from the message (phone, address, name, etc.) and save the record.

RELATIONSHIP PROSPECTING ONLINE

Just as real estate professionals relationship prospect offline, they must, to take advantage of the new cyberculture, relationship prospect online by joining and participating in various forms of online communities.

Participating on the Internet over long periods of time allows you to build lasting relationships. Participating in real estate forums provides the opportunity to demonstrate expertise that will help increase the trust and confidence that the group and its members have in you. If the community is a group of real estate professionals, your participation will increase the odds of your receiving a referral from another member of the community. Individual members of the community will feel, to a degree, that they know you. That is one of the benefits of being an active participant in RealTalk.

When you participate in consumer real estate forums, you can promise to get back to community members with specific real estate information when they ask for it. You are making a promise and keeping it; once again, a tool for building trust and confidence. You can find good generic content you can use without fear of copyright violation at *http://InternetCrusade.com.* Access the real estate glossary, real estate fundamentals, and the buying and selling real estate information for use in your online community-building adventures.

You possess specific knowledge about your city or part of the country, information that is not in any book or in any newspaper. This knowledge is the history of the community that you, as a real estate professional, can relate to Internet prospects better than anyone. Share that specialized information on the Internet and build a presence as the expert in your area.

■ FINDING ONLINE COMMUNITIES

There are many special interest communities that you can join and begin to develop a presence in. Finding these communities can be simple, if you know how. Most of the major search engines will return a wealth of information if you

> **■ TIP**
> Go to http://Google.com and search for a few of your interests.

search with the right terminology. As a start, there is a good list of Listserv links, found by searching the Google search engine. Use these lists and the following ideas to help you get connected to the communities that have content in which you are interested and/or have some expertise.

CREATING ONLINE COMMUNITIES

How about participating in (or starting) an alumni association Listserv community?

You can find real estate groups on America Online, Yahoo, and other portals. Create community Listservs—start a local Kiwanis, Rotary, church, or Boy Scout Listserv community. Be a community organizer.

http://CreatingOnlineCommunities.RealTown.com

■ COMMUNITY PARTICIPATION; GENERAL CONCEPTS

If you participate or want to begin to participate in online communities, keep the following in mind:

- Build an online persona. Think about your posts—read them twice before hitting Send. Avoiding the use of pronouns will make your post more readable and understandable.
- Set your mail software to plain text (not HTML) when participating in Listserv digests.

- Be helpful and share.
- Learn to handle and manipulate information from various sources on the Web and observe copyright law.
- Learn where people congregate on the Internet and for what reason.
- How do you prospect now? Do you spend time as a member of a club or group? Relationship and referral (special interest, community)-based marketing requires a commitment of time, be it in the real world or online.
- Establish discipline. Spend 30 minutes per day participating in online communities learning more about the Internet and technology, and meeting new people. Some of this participation can be delegated to assistants, but you might like it and be good at it so don't rule out that possibility.
- Participate in the RealTalk community. The more you post to RealTalk, the more exposure and Internet presence you will gain, and the more likely you will receive referrals from other real estate professionals.

■ BEING A GOOD COMMUNITY CITIZEN

As a member of a virtual community, you have responsibilities to the community. Read the posts and reply with clear, well thought-out responses. Compose new messages of relevance to the group.

At your option, it is OK to lurk (stay back in the shadows without adding your posts) during your first month or so of Listserv membership. This enables you to read enough of the messages so that you develop a sense of the tempo and the knowledge level of the group mind. Listserv communities develop a collective group consciousness and, in many cases, the sum of the knowledge in the group is greater than the sum of the individual parts—this is digital synergy.

COMMUNITY DO'S AND DON'TS

When participating in online communities, do:

- involve yourself—the community wants and needs your unique talent, perspective, and knowledge;
- keep an open mind—allowing others to be wrong;
- listen and learn;

- be open and honest;
- be concise, especially with your signature; it is generally accept-able to have up to five lines for your personal signature, and any more is probably advertising and will add length to posts;
- be clear about the subject in the message subject line; and
- become a better communicator as a result of the practice you get participating in the community—improve your writing skills to make your point.

When participating in online communities, don't:

- flame other members of the community;
- USE ALL CAPS—it is considered shouting on the Internet;
- reply to a message without telling the group what your reply relates to—usually you will copy some brief amount of the original message for reference, separated by quotes or brackets;
- reply to a message leaving the entire original message intact—the result of quoting the entire message is a long and cumbersome digest;
- send messages in HTML format—digests cannot handle them effectively, although they are acceptable on immediate delivery listservs;
- republish any message sent to you privately that expresses a desire not to be published;
- republish a message with a copyright unless permission is given prior to the post;
- use an address that has an auto-responder attached to it;
- require a "Read Receipt" to your postings—it is considered a way to steal the list of participants' addresses, which is frowned upon as a member of the community and it will also subject you to multiple receipts (you will receive a receipt for every person who reads each message you post).
- hog the stage—do let other members share their experiences. You don't have to comment on every message posted; save your best for those issues most important to you. The most effective Listservs are the ones that publish good content, as opposed to the one-line chat-room variety. "High-content, low-noise" describes the ideal Listserv.

■ VIRTUAL REAL ESTATE COMMUNITIES

For a list of online real estate communities go to: *http://ListOf Communities.RealTown.com.*

FREE ONLINE COMMUNITIES FOR ASSOCIATIONS AND AFFILIATES

InternetCrusade offers free listservs to associations, WCR chapters, and nonprofit organizations. For information on setting up a listserv for your organization send an e-mail to *ListServ@Internet Crusade.com.*

For more information on managing an online Listserv community go to: *http://ListservManual.RealTown.com.*

Chapter Links:
http://RealTalk.RealTown.com
http://BestOfRealTalk.RealTown.com
http://Google.com
http://CreatingOnlineCommunities.RealTown.com
http://ListOfCommunities.RealTown.com
http://ListservManual.RealTown.com

■ REVIEW QUESTIONS

1. (T/F) Participating in an online community can be a profitable experience and can be a cost-effective use of your time.

   Answer: True.

   Major benefits from participation in online communities include referrals from other real estate professionals, leads for listings and sales, a resource for information at your fingertips, and collective power with vendors.

2. List some of the reasons vendors monitor and participate in online communities.

   Answer: Vendors are often members of industry-specific online communities or receive copies of the messages exchanged within the community about their products and services. Often, they elect to respond. In some cases their response is an explanation to clear up a misunderstanding or miscommunication. At times, complaints are addressed and refuted. The vendor also has the opportunity to take immediate action to resolve the issue and report the resolution to the community members! Vendors who promptly address the needs and concerns of their customers gain by developing a product and brand loyalty from the community members.

3. List three online community formats; describe them.

Answer: Listservs: e-mail lists, which are very effective because most people visit their e-mail inbox multiple times a day.

Bulletin Boards: A place on the WWW where members go to post ideas and thoughts, contributions.

Chat: This requires all participants to be online at the same time—typically, to have a conversation.

Chapter Fifteen

Technology Training

Learn from the past, set vivid, detailed goals for the future, and live in the only moment of time over which you have any control: now.
DENIS WAITLEY
http://Motivation.RealTown.com

Fundamental training in the **operating system** is the key to effective computing. Familiarity with the operating system will give you a head start on all other applications. Technology can be learned live or online, and ongoing technology assistance can be obtained through online user groups such as RealTalk and eProTalk. In addition, standard real estate courses such as ethics and agency are now offered in an online environment.

All technology has a learning curve for the user. To get the most out of computer software, it is important to realize that a certain amount of time must be invested; moreover, the more you use the software, the more you will benefit from its use.

■ WINDOWS FAMILIARITY

There are millions of Windows users, making it the most widely used operating system for personal computing in the world. Given this popularity, it becomes critically important that the new real estate professional become as familiar as possible with Windows. There are those ardent Mac users and we salute them for their loyalty. Nevertheless, in today's world, most software is written for Windows, so it makes good sense to go with the flow when it comes to selecting an operating system.

The more you know about the Windows operating system, the easier it will be for you to benefit from technology. You wouldn't start driving around in an unfamiliar car without testing the brakes, adjusting the seat and mirrors, or trying out the radio. So why buy or start using a computer without testing a few of its components?

Windows is a software program—different from other software or applications in that it is the computer's operating system, like the engine is for your car. There are many other software programs that allow you to perform word processing, send/receive e-mail, surf the Internet, or perform financial functions. Windows allows you to install and interact with those other programs.

Part of the power of software is that most tasks can be accomplished in a number of ways. For example, you can close a software program by clicking the "X" in the upper right corner or by clicking the File menu and selecting Exit. There are other ways of accomplishing the same task. Theoretically, the fewer keystrokes (and clicks) it takes to accomplish a task, the more efficiently you are using the software. So clicking the "X" is the easiest and fastest with fewer clicks. Keyboard shortcuts are another way to reduce keystrokes and clicks. Always keep in mind that there really is no wrong way. If you get the results you are looking for, that is all that matters. There may be a faster way, which, to some, may seem better, but the best way is the way you are comfortable doing it.

> **■ TIP**
> Point your cursor to your desktop and right click where there is nothing on your desktop. Notice the pop up menu. Every chance you get, right click and examine the options.

The more familiar you are with the Windows operating system the easier it will be to master other software. If you haven't done so already, take some Windows training. You'll find a variety of courses available online as well as in the classroom. During a Windows training class you should be exposed to the fundamentals of using the operating system and its components. Courses are available at community colleges, computer stores, and local real estate associations. Try your best to become Windows proficient.

■ KEYBOARD SHORTCUTS

Open a new window in the current application.	Ctrl+N
Save the current document.	Ctrl+S
Copy the selected area.	Ctrl+C
Paste the contents of the clipboard.	Ctrl+V
Cut the selected area.	Ctrl+X
Undo (most applications).	Ctrl+Z
Open an existing file.	Ctrl+O
Print the current document.	Ctrl+P
Close the current document.	Ctrl+W
Quit the current application.	Ctrl+Q
Bookmark the current page (Netscape and IE only).	Ctrl+D
Switch between open windows quickly.	Alt+Tab
Terminate an application that won't respond.	Ctrl+Alt+Del
Shut down a system that won't respond.	Ctrl+Alt+Del

■ ONLINE CLASSES

There are many online learning opportunities available today offering speed, convenience, and choice to the real estate professional. From basic real estate classes in ethics and agency to technology classes, it can all be done online. For many, once they have tried an online course, it becomes their preference.

HEWLETT-PACKARD LEARNING CENTER

Hewlett-Packard offers, through their HP Learning Center, a wide range of informational courses as varied as your interests—in a unique interactive learning environment. Their courses are taught by experts, authors, and leaders in these areas.

All HP Learning Center courses are listed at *http://HPLearning Center.com.* Click on the course title to get an overview including a short course description, the instructor's objectives for the class, and any prerequisites that may be necessary.

At this writing, courses at HP Learning Center are free of charge and anyone is welcome to enroll.

REALTOR® UNIVERSITY

REALTOR® University is the National Association of REALTORS® Internet-based education delivery system where real estate professionals can take courses online for continuing education credit, professional development, and designation certification.

KAPLAN COLLEGE

Kaplan Professional Schools provide real estate and financial services licensing and continuing education programs through live classroom instruction, Internet-based learning, and correspondence courses to help professionals acquire the

> ■ **TIP**
> Take your next continuing education class online.

skills needed to meet state licensing and educational requirements. In addition, the schools offer programs for sales agents, brokers, appraisers, home inspectors, and contractors. The schools include Anthony Schools in California; The Leonard-Hawes Real Estate Schools in Texas; Jones College in Colorado; The Dearborn Real Estate Institute in New Mexico; Prosource Educational Services, Inc., in Minnesota; and Inspection Training Associates in California, Connecticut, Florida, Illinois, and Virginia.

For more information go to *http://OnlineLearning.RealTown.com.*

■ BECOME AN E-PRO

http://ePro.RealTown.com

NAR's e-PRO—Online Technology Training and Certification

After a false start with the initial provider, NAR turned to a long established technology solution provider and consulting firm to bring the second version of e-PRO to the industry. The current **e-PRO Certification Program** was developed by InternetCrusade, a Hawaii Corporation doing business in San Diego and a technology solution provider and consultant to the real estate industry since 1995. This is a program created by REALTORS® for REALTORS® to prepare real estate professionals to make the most of the Internet and other technologies as they serve today's connected consumer. One of NAR's key initiatives is to impress upon its members the importance of embracing technology and how it can be used to enhance their success. More than 10,000 members have signed up for e-PRO.

It is time to reformulate your compelling argument. With all the options available to consumers today, and the downward pressure on commissions, what is your compelling argument? Why should a consumer hire you for their real estate needs? The answer can be found in the response to the following question:

If you could hire anyone in your city to work with to sell real estate you own or to help you acquire property, why would you hire you? The e-PRO Certification will help you formulate your answer to that critical question.

MAIN THEMES OF THE E-PRO COURSE

1. It's the little things that make a difference. A study by NAR tells us that the number of buyers and sellers shopping online for a home and for a real estate agent is on the rise. Based on a survey of online buyers by the California Association of REALTORS®, online buyers typically make more money and buy more expensive homes than conventional buyers. Online buyers are truly a niche worth cultivating.

Often real estate professionals will let the fact that technology comprises such a large body of knowledge and information intimidate them and prevent them from taking action. They avoid technology solutions because they believe technology is an all or nothing proposition. This is not the case. Little points and tips included in one's day-to-day practice can, and often do, have a positive impact on the bottom line. Many real estate professionals are afraid to create and implement a technology plan of action, giving those with a plan a distinct advantage. Module 4 of the e-PRO course of instruction works with students to create their own personal Technology Plan of Action.

2. It's easy when you know how. Don't you just hate it when you ask a technology question and you get the condescending reply "That's easy"? It makes you wish you never asked. The fact is, most of the things you want to do with technology are just three or four clicks away—you just need someone to show you the right clicks. After that, it is easy. The e-PRO program will give you access to technology and real estate professionals who are willing to share information you can use in your business, and your membership in this **online community** continues after you complete the course of instruction and are certified—and there is no annual fee.

3. Differentiate yourself from the competition. Real estate is a "me too" business. Even real estate agent and broker marketing is "me too." Over 90 percent of the work performed by residential real estate professionals is the same after obtaining the listing (place listing in the MLS, put up a for sale sign, put a lock box on the property, run classified ads, and hold open house). Technology gives you a great opportunity to differentiate yourself from your competition.

Have you ever known an agent to give out note pads/magnets/calendars/flyswatters/rain caps/etc.? Any new marketing idea is quickly copied by others, as this is a "me too" business. Most agents have Web sites and use sold riders—it is all "me too." Have you ever been on a listing appointment and watched the seller take notes on one of the pads given to them by one of your competitors as you glance across the kitchen to the refrigerator and notice all the magnets of agents long out of the business?

What can you do that is different and that will make you stand out from the crowd? E-PRO is the answer. There are more than 950,000 REALTORS® and only 10,000 e-PROs.

4. Integrate technology into what you are already doing. Technology will not replace the real estate professional. Nor is technology alone the answer to survival in a changing business. Successful real estate professionals will look at their business and figure out ways to integrate technology into what they are already doing to make them more effective and efficient.

5. Raising the bar without leaving anyone behind. E-PRO is designed to ensure that all who enroll graduate from the program. It is state-of-the-art online learning coupled with the personal touch of instructor and student contact through the development of the e-PRO online community.

The following outlines construction of the course content and the technology delivery platform:

- Candidates have a six-month enrollment period to complete the course, which takes about 20 to 30 hours.
- The course is taught entirely online.

- The course teaches to all levels, from novice to technology expert; the course was designed to bring something to everyone and receives glowing testimonials daily.
- There is no annual fee and e-PRO is an elective for the CRS, CPM, and ABR designations. It is also approved for continuing education in a number of states (see *http://eProNAR.com* CE Approval).
- Access to e-PRO Community is available through listserv discussion forums.

E-PRO COURSE PRESENTATION

The e-PRO course is presented in four modules; each module contains four sections. The technology allows for 3,000 simultaneous users per second, is administered through a Web interface accessed at *http://eProNAR.com* from any computer with Internet access, and includes the following components:

Text reading material. The text reading material incorporates review questions to make sure the student is following the material; questions are asked every 500 words or so. If a student misses the answer, the student is told why and allowed to answer the question again before being allowed to move forward in the course.

Virtual Field Trips. Students are sent to various Web sites to learn to better utilize the resources of the Internet and the World Wide Web. They are then asked to answer discussion questions about what they discovered on the field trips. The answers to these and other assignments are later reviewed by an instructor when the coursework is validated.

Section Exams. Each section has a 12-question exam following the readings and the field trips. A score of 75 percent is required to move forward and if the student is unable to score 75 percent the student is allowed to retake the exam until a passing score of 75 percent or better is obtained. The questions are pulled randomly from a pool of questions for each section. Each question teaches or relates to a learning objective of the course ("raising the bar without leaving anyone behind").

Final Exam. A 50-question exam is administered, requiring a 75 percent passing grade. If a student does not obtain 75 percent, the student is allowed to retake the exam until a 75 percent or better is obtained.

There is also an e-mail component to allow students to become more familiar with their e-mail software and functionality. There is a Listserv discussion forum for each module giving the student contact with instructors, current students, and graduates—a true national support network for technology as well as a place to ask questions and receive answers.

COURSE CONTENT

Module 1—Understanding the Miracle of the Internet. In this module, students learn about the technology challenge and making the technology investment.

Module 2—Becoming an E-Mail Powerhouse. Many people believe they have mastered e-mail when in fact, e-mail is software and few people master any software. Think about your ability to use word processing software. Are you able to do everything the software was designed to do? The first concept of word processing software often is that it is a replacement for the typewriter. That paradigm or concept keeps many from maximizing the power of word processing software. Most people's paradigm or concept of e-mail is "send and receive." This limits the power e-mail can bring to your business.

Module 3—World Wide Web—Marketing, Publishing, Service, and Support. An Internet presence is made up of an e-mail presence and a Web presence. Just as your domain is the foundation of your e-mail presence (You@YourBrand.com), your domain is the center of your Web presence as well. The address of your Web site, the URL (Uniform Resource Locator) should contain your domain *(http://YourBrand.com)*.

Module 4—Tying It All Together—Tools of the Trade, Virtual Community, and Technology Plan of Action. The delivery platform for ePRO includes features and fail-safes that allow for its use to present any type of information (and in any language) while at the same time being able to monitor and control the flow of all the data in real time.

E-PRO Scholarships. A number of vendors have recognized the importance of technology training for today's real estate professional by participating in the e-PRO scholarship program. Using a variety of criteria, they have provided full tuition e-PRO scholarships. To date, Rapattoni Corporation has awarded the most scholarships—see *http://eproscholarships.internetcrusade.com*. Other participants include eNeighborhoods, HomeFeedback, VisualTour, HomeGain, and Supra.

E-PRO CE APPROVAL

The e-PRO course is approved for continuing education credit in several states. Check the list of states and the hours allowed by going to *http://eProNAR.com* and clicking on the CE Approval button. The course has been accredited by ARELLO for distance learning certification. In addition, CRS, CPM, and ABR allow the e-PRO course to substitute for one of their elective course requirements.

Chapter Links:
http://OnlineLearning.RealTown.com
http://ePro.RealTown.com

■ REVIEW QUESTIONS

1. List three sources for online learning.

   Answer:

   HP Learning Center
   eProNAR.com
   Dearborn.com

2. Understanding which software is the key to successful computing?

   Answer: Windows

3. What is one of the themes of the e-PRO certification?

   Answer:

   Raising the bar, without leaving anyone behind
   It's easy when you know how
   It's the little things that make a difference
   Integrate technology into what you are already doing
   Created by REALTORS® for REALTORS®

Chapter Sixteen

Technology Tools for Real Estate Professionals

Make a list of your current wants and desires. Next to each, put down what benefit or payoff there would be when you achieve it. Look at this list often throughout the day and before retiring at night.

DENIS WAITLEY
http://Motivation.InternetCrusade.com

Today's real estate professional has a new challenge: keeping up with the different technology tools available. The upgrading of old tools and the creation of new tools complicates the issue. This chapter has been designed to bring you information about the most utilized technologies and provide you with a reference for future use.

■ DIGITAL CAMERAS

For more information on this subject go to:
http://DigitalCameras.RealTown.com

One of the most important advances in digital technology for the real estate industry has been the creation and evolution of the **digital camera**—both still and video types. Until the availability of high quality, reasonably priced digital cameras, real estate professionals had to rely on conventional **analog** cameras and **scanners** to get images of listed properties out on the Web. Now, with a digital camera and a relatively simple application program, real estate professionals of all levels of technical sophistication can make high-quality pictures, videos, and virtual tours available to potential buyers, almost in an instant.

Buyers continue to indicate their preference for multiple property images on the Internet. As a matter of fact, your listings probably have a better chance of being the request of buyers if you use more pictures to showcase the listings.

You might wonder how a digital camera works. Like a traditional analog camera, the digital camera is little more than a recording device for light. Look through the viewer, click, and the image you see passes through the lens and is recorded. The major difference is how and where the picture is recorded. In the conventional camera, it is recorded by being almost burned into film. The film is light sensitive. Whatever amount and type (brilliance, contrast, color balance) of light comes through the aperture affects how the image is chemically burned into the film.

In the digital camera, the image still enters through the aperture as light. The image is read by the microprocessor (light-sensing), which translates it into **digital data** and records it onto a more-or-less permanent storage medium. There are a number of ways the image is stored.

Whatever media the camera uses for storage, it is then a matter of transferring the digitized image into a computer for transmission to the Internet host or e-mail, or to use in a publication. This process is easiest if you have the type of camera with **floppy disk** or compact disc storage because of the compatibility with your PC's components. Of course, pictures can be great or they can be poor. The key to success in photography is to take lots of pictures using different angles and levels of light. In doing so, you have a better chance of getting a few good ones. With conventional photography, this can be costly. With digital photography you can take as many as you want. View the image immediately and decide if the image is one you want to use. If not, you can simply erase it and try another.

DIGITAL CAMERAS IN REAL ESTATE

A digital camera also gives you the opportunity to interact with the buyer or seller. Have you ever had sellers who were dissatisfied with the pictures you took of their property? Has the picture of one of your listings submitted to the MLS ever disappointed you? If you are like most real estate professionals, the answer is probably "yes" to both questions. Let the sellers take their own pictures with your digital camera for the flyers, newsletters, ads—get them involved.

For buyers, take your digital camera with you on showings, taking pictures of the properties as appropriate for your buyer customers or clients. You can then give them a showing summary with pictures on a disk or e-mailed to them. (Before e-mailing **digital images,** make sure that the recipient is expecting them and that they are connected at a high enough speed to avoid any inconvenience. It might be easier to load the photos onto a Web page and send the buyers a link.) Having a camera that saves photos as .jpg images is ideal. A jpeg (pronounced "jay-peg" (.jpg) image is much smaller in file size than the .bmp images other cameras may save their photos in. The will require much less formatting of your photos in the long run.

As nature does not like to cooperate sometimes, you may find that pictures need to be enhanced by lightening them. With other photos you may need to crop, shrink, filter, or otherwise enhance them. In the event you need to, there are many tools available—from novice to expert.

WHAT ARE SOME OF THE PRACTICAL BUSINESS APPLICATIONS OF A DIGITAL CAMERA?

The digital camera is fast becoming a critical tool for the successful real estate professional. Here is a list of real estate applications. Can you think of any more?

- For Sale flyers with color photos printed as a single document
- Personal brochure—complete with photos
- Virtual Tour—house
- Virtual Tour—area/street
- Family electronic portrait for closing gift
- Before and after home showing pictures (getting the home ready for presentation/open house)
- Enhance your online listings and easily take multiple photos for MLS
- Add new images to your Web site daily
- Keep a "Neighborhood Journal" file complete with pictures
- Create a community tour Web site for relocation purposes, with pictures of the city/town and major attractions
- Keep photos of your property inspection of all listings
- Listing presentations—showing the potential client how their home will look in marketing brochures
- Move-in tenant inspection

FIGURE 16.1 ■ Digital Camera Use

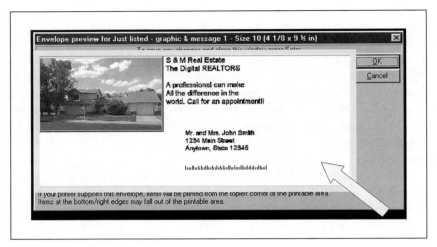

Screen shot reprinted by permission from Microsoft Corporation.

- Move-out tenant inspection
- FSBO/expired letters (envelopes)

As you can see, there are so many valuable uses for a digital camera in the residential real estate industry. We have only scratched the surface here, as there are more and more applications of this great technology coming along every day.

■ VIRTUAL TOURS

For more information on this subject go to http://VirtualTours.RealTown.com.

Imagine that you want your buyer prospects to walk through a new property listing. You want them to see the rooms, feel the sizes, notice the flow from room to room—but they live out of the area. "They would love this house," you think. But by the time they are scheduled to visit your area for house-hunting purposes, this house will certainly be sold. Or maybe the buyers live nearby, but it's tough to get both spouses together today to see this listing. What can you do to help them and help you show them the house in time to make a decision?

Now, imagine being able to show hundreds of potential buyers the best features of your listings at literally any time, day or night, without having to actually visit the property.

Well, as far-fetched as it might seem to the uninitiated, this is a perfect opportunity for a virtual tour. A virtual tour is a series of 360° wide angle panoramic or still photos combined with captions, and in some cases unlimited text descriptions and a streaming voice narration that can be viewed over the Internet. These virtual tours are typically linked directly to your online listing on your Web site and other Web sites where your listing is exposed (your MLS, *Realtor.com*, Yahoo!, etc.) There are two primary ways to create virtual tours, and each has its advantages and disadvantages. They are full service and agent created.

FULL SERVICE VIRTUAL TOURS

Full service virtual tours are created for you by a local service provider in your area.

Full Service Tours—Advantages. There are several advantages to full service tours.

- It's simple—you just pick up the phone and call.
- No technical expertise or training is required to create the tour.
- No equipment is required for you to own or use.
- No time is required on your part to create the tour (however, normally you do have to spend time meeting the photographer to take the pictures).

Full Service Tours—Disadvantages. There are several disadvantages to full service tours:

- You have almost no control over the look and content of the tour. The photographer can only show large rooms or outside views that display well as a 360° scene.
- There is no differentiation for you; the tour you order is fairly generic and it will look the same for any listing agent who orders it.
- Most of these tours brand the virtual tour company; no branding or personal promotion is provided to the agent. This is the equivalent of putting a yard sign at your listing that just says "For Sale—sign provided by XYZ sign company."
- While you don't need any technical expertise to create the tour, you won't have any direct results because of the tour's existence. You'll need some technical involvement to ensure that the tour is

displayed on your own Web site and that you have the ability to capture leads from the tour or be contacted from homebuyers who see the tour.

- The expense is a disadvantage. As you're paying someone else, most agents limit their use of virtual tours to just high-end listings, or when a seller demands this service. Having additional scenes or new photos taken drives up the cost further.

AGENT CREATED VIRTUAL TOURS

Today's more marketing-savvy agent now has another choice in virtual tours that offers a number of significant advantages over the traditional service provider-created tour. Agent created tours do have some disadvantages, however.

Agent Created Tour—Advantages. There are several advantages to agent created tours:

- You are in complete control of the tour. You use *your* sales skills to present the listing. Your tours aren't simply a series of a few scenes with captions like your competitors. You're using your sales skills to show the listing over the Internet.
- Customer interaction is improved. Imagine the home sellers whom you engage in your presentation when they follow you from room to room to discuss which angle to display in your tours. And think about the powerful impact you'll have when you tell them the virtual tour you create will be on your Web site and e-mailed to buyers tonight—not a week from now.
- The tour is far less expensive. Most agent created virtual tours are a small fraction of the cost of full service virtual tours. This cost savings means that you can afford to use virtual tours more often—on every listing. This can be a key advantage in your listing and marketing strategy.
- The tour provides more and better content (up to 50 scenes per tour with unlimited text). Buyers enjoy looking at the smaller rooms and neighborhood. Why not show this to them with non-360° scenes that are more appropriate? And you won't have that distorted or warped effect you see in so many 360° only virtual tours.
- There is a no need to schedule a photographer—you photograph the listing when it's convenient for you and the seller, and you

can modify the photos and tour content as needed at no additional cost.

- There is a much faster time to market—you can create and post the tour the same day as you get the listing without having to wait for a photographer.
- There are no geographic limitations—you don't have to worry about whether there's a photographer in your area.
- You have the ability to use different types of scenes (full 360°, panoramic, or still images) instead of being limited to just 360° scenes. For example, you may want to exclude an expensive painting from a wide angle panoramic scene. You can't do this if you're limited to showing only full 360° scenes.
- You have the ability to add streaming voice to the tour.
- You have the ability to add hotspots to the tour to allow the viewer to jump from area to area by clicking on doorways, windows, etc.
- You have the ability to change the tour at any time after it's posted to the Internet.
- You have the ability as a buyer's agent to create tours for out-of-town buyers of other agent's listings.
- You have the ability to include other types of images in the tour (e.g., floor plans, logos, etc.)
- It is possible to reuse the photos. With this solution, you can use your digital photos for many other marketing purposes such as flyers, postcards, MLS entries, and magazine ads. You can't do this with the 360° images from full service virtual tours.

Agent Created Tour—Disadvantages. There are several disadvantages to the agent created tour:

- You'll need to have a Windows PC and a digital camera to use.
- You'll need to spend an hour or two learning a new software application to create your tours.
- You'll spend some time at the listing taking photos and another 20 to 30 minutes using the software to create a tour. Compare this with the time you would spend scheduling an outside photographer, meeting the photographer a second time at the listing, and watching the photographer take photos.

■ PERSONAL DIGITAL ASSISTANT/ PERSONAL INFORMATION MANAGER—PDA/PIM

For more information on this subject go to *http://PersonalDigital Assistants.RealTown.com.*

Personal Digital Assistant/PIM (Personal Information Manager) is a name that aptly describes this technology, which offers a wealth of flexibility to real estate professionals. This genre of tools probably began in 1993 with the introduction of the Apple Newton—a handheld organizer with the ability of beaming information to other Newton users and synchronizing data with a desktop computer. The Newton quickly gained a loyal following, mostly among an early adopter user base (corporate programmers, product marketing, product management, and middle management). Unfortunately, Apple once again kept their technology close to the vest and did not license the Newton operating system to third parties until it was almost too late. That was in 1998, after the Palm Pilot was introduced to tremendous success and Newton saw its market share falling away. That year, Newton was discontinued.

Users from sales, marketing, small business, students, and others were initially attracted to Palm's clean, small design and wealth of application tools (calendar, address book, to-do, memo, expense, and mail) all with an easy-to-use **synchronization** with the desktop computer.

Within a year of Palm Pilot's obvious success, the floodgates opened as new products and configurations of handheld computers were introduced to the market. Today, Palm still has the dominant market share, but the others are rapidly gaining ground.

Handspring, created by the two original founders of Palm and using the Palm operating system, is the fastest growing among these. The Handspring added the availability of a hot-port for adding feature-specific module cards, such as memory, cell phone, etc.

Noted among the competitors to the Palm OS-based handhelds are those based on the Windows for Pocket PC operating system. Notables among the Pocket PC ranks are the HP Jornada, the Casio Cassiopeia, and the Compaq iPAQ. This operating system offers users the advantage of running palm-sized versions of (Microsoft Office) tools—for example, Pocket Word and Pocket Excel. Palm, on the other hand, is combating this with the availability of third-party applications, like the DataViz Desktop to Go and Documents to Go application family.

Both the Pocket PC and the Palm-based handhelds do a good job of synching data between the desktop computer and the handheld. Using these religiously, you could effectively take the most important information with you out into the field.

WHAT CAN I DO WITH A PDA; WHICH HANDHELD IS THE BEST?

There is no answer to this question. As we often say: "The best is the one that you will use." Your preference will be based on several considerations:

- Available software—Does it link to your MLS? Does it synch to your PIM?
- Design and function—Does it fit your hand? Does it look good? Do you like it?
- Cost—A **no-brainer**
- **Wow factor**—How cool is it? Yes, wow factor is important. After all of the other considerations are met—you like it, it fits the need, it fits the budget—it still needs to be impressive. That is just a fact of life. You will want prospects, clients, and associates to say, "She knows what she is doing!" To learn more about handhelds and compare the features and cost of all handhelds, you should visit Handango and ZDNet's Handheld Super Center.

At the heart of every handheld is the PIM (Personal Information Manager) tool base. This includes:

- date book;
- contacts;
- activities (to-do);
- memos;
- calculator; and
- expenses.

These applications are fairly simple to use and can be auto-synched to your desktop information in Outlook, ACT, Goldmine, and many other commercially available Personal Information Managers.

In addition to this useful tool set, recent developments offer these abilities (an option with added software):

- Synch to Top Producer and AgentOffice
- Download your MLS (see Pocket Real Estate and Supra)
- Show PowerPoint Slide Shows

The power and storage size of these tools is growing almost daily. They are touted to eventually replace the notebook PC for the majority of away-from-the-office uses.

With the advent of **wireless communications,** you will be able to check your e-mail, look up listings, send a message, get directions, and (due to **hybridization** between cell phones and handhelds) make calls from almost anywhere without a hard-wired connection!

■ PERSONAL PRODUCTIVITY SOFTWARE

For more information on this subject go to: *http://PersonalProductivitySoftware.RealTown.com.*

CONTACT MANAGERS AND PERSONAL INFORMATION MANAGERS

For the purposes of this topic, discussion will focus on business and contact management systems (often called customer relationship manager, CRM, or PIM solutions). These range from the simple handheld calculator applications to the elegant and often-overwhelming contact management systems. No one in sales should operate without a time management or personal productivity system. For years it was Day Timer, Franklin Planner, Day Runner, and others. Today it can all be done on your computer—and for those of you who still feel good carrying around paper, have no fear, just hit "Print."

The following products are real estate industry-specific business and contact management systems:

- Top Producer
- AgentOffice
- PREP

They would compare to similar products that are not specific to this real estate industry:

- ACT!
- Goldmine
- Microsoft Outlook

At their core, each of the above listed products does a very good job of helping you acquire, assemble, and use information about one of your biggest assets as a real estate professional: your sphere of influence. This includes friends, family, prospects, clients, customers, associates, vendors, and homeowners in your farm.

Personal productivity applications help you store and manage all of the information that you can possibly obtain about any of the people you might possibly know, meet, work with, service, get services from, or otherwise contact in your life. Remember, memory is cheap.

Such applications allow you to market in a consistent, efficient, and cost-effective way. You have all of the information about any given person at your fingertips at the click of the mouse. These programs also offer very powerful scheduling tools that help you to manage your time, track tasks (to-do lists), schedule regular contacts with clients, schedule meetings, manage calls, organize mailings, and more.

Most of these tools also give you the ability to track the history of your experiences with each and every person with whom you come in contact. Notes of conversations, copies of correspondence (printed and electronic), activities on their behalf, and more can easily be tracked, searched, and displayed instantly. The capability to search correspondence and a client record is the foundation of risk management and the use of these types of applications is a great risk reduction technique.

The applications usually include features such as e-mail, **auto-dialers,** word processing, and some form of mass-marketing tool. This is where the generic, open-market products usually stop.

The industry-specific tools, Top Producer, AgentOffice, PREP, and others pick up from there and integrate real estate applications that might make them more attractive to the new real estate professional. Such tools include:

- automatic color property flyers;
- Web-enabled property pages;
- Web-enabled news feeds;
- Internet-capable CMAs;
- buyer/seller/transaction monitoring;
- listing/closing tracking; and
- extensive income property statistics.

The three industry-specific tools mentioned here offer synchronization through their desktop software with the more popular handheld devices, so that you can have your business information with you at all times.

WHICH PRODUCTIVITY SOFTWARE IS BEST FOR YOU?

As always, the best one is the one that you will use. It makes little sense to spend hundreds of dollars on a full-feature solution, invest countless hours getting your detailed information loaded, and then not use it in a dedicated fashion. These products are only as good as the use you give them. All too often, the dedication required to integrate electronic tools like these into an established business practice can seem daunting and not worth the perceived effort. Veteran professionals might feel that it is just too much effort for too little gain, and give up early or even before they start. As a result, business and personal productivity software sometimes collects dust on the shelf. Don't bite off more than you can chew. The generic tools are less expensive and have less of a learning curve.

So look at your time and needs, then make your choice. It takes time for this type of tool to become an integral part of your practice. If you take the time, you will gain measurably in terms of efficiency, professionalism, and confidence. It is something that you should attack with fervor, now that you are becoming a new real estate professional!

■ ELECTRONIC LOCK BOX

For more information on this subject go to *http:// LockBox.Real-Town.com.*

As an industry, we have evolved from using a key-type system, to a combination key/combo, to the combo-only conventional lock box. Today these are generally being upgraded to systems that will allow the professional to use electronic lock boxes. Many MLSs across the country have converted to electronic lock boxes.

Currently, the dominant lock box provider is Supra. Supra introduced their first electronic lock box, the Advantage Express, in 1990. A few years later, Supra unveiled the Supra iBox, an electronic lock box that uses infrared technology. Both lock boxes use an electronic key.

Other lock box providers are Rapattoni and Sentrylocks (a partner of the National Association of REALTORS®).

Electronic lock boxes interface with PDAs and provide a wide range of data for the real estate professional.

■ REDUCING PAPERWORK WITH DIGITAL DOCUMENT MANAGEMENT (DDM)

As a real estate professional, you know how easy it is to get lost in the shuffle of paperwork required to complete a real estate transaction. Multiple revisions of multiple documents from multiple parties all add up to multiple errors and a lot of wasted time. Here's the good news— paperwork is quickly becoming a thing of the past in the real estate industry. Advances in technology and online business are reinventing the process of managing even the most complex real estate transactions.

Software packages like ZipForm (WINForms in California), the official forms software of the National Association of REALTORS® (NAR), are designed to digitally manage an entire library of both custom and standard real estate forms, as well as keep track of individual real estate transactions.

Not only does managing documents digitally save time and money, it also allows you to collaborate seamlessly and share documents with other parties involved in the transaction—clients, lenders, title, and closing agents.

The key to digital document management (DDM) lies in data integration capabilities. With ZipForm, for example, data is entered once and automatically shared among all the documents related to a single transaction. When any changes are made to one document, all other documents are automatically updated with the new information. This saves untold hours of rekeying and reduces the mess and error potential involved in making changes. Another contract form software in the marketplace is produced by RealFast.

In addition to reducing the amount of administrative time spent working with documents and dramatically reducing administrative errors, DDM offers even more benefits to the real estate professional. Using DDM at this point in the evolution of technology and the real estate transaction allows you to differentiate yourself from the competition. You get a leading and competitive advantage over those who still employ traditional paperwork methods while saving time and money and increasing productivity.

With DDM, real estate professionals also have the advantages of:

- e-mail/PDF capabilities that enable virtual document review without compromising the security of the original document;
- quick and easy storage and retrieval of documents;

- reduced liability of keeping track of copies of complete transaction paperwork; and
- accessibility that enables agents and brokers to access files from remote locations.

http://DigitalDocumentManagement.RealTown.com

■ PDF—Document Portability

Want to send a contract or a lease agreement and not worry about the content being changed? PDF may provide the solution. PDF is the standard for the secure and reliable distribution and exchange of electronic documents and forms around the world.

PDF stands for Portable Document Format. It is a universal file format that preserves the fonts, images, graphics, and layout of any document, regardless of the application and platform used to create it.

Adobe PDF files are compact and complete, and can be shared, viewed, and printed by anyone with free Adobe Reader software. For more information on Adobe and PDF go to *http://PDF.RealTown.com*.

■ INTERNET-BASED MLS

For more information on this subject go to *http://MLSInformation.RealTown.com*.

Internet access to MLS data has seemingly been slow in coming to those who have watched this sector for the past few years. Products have come and products not able to gain enough market share have fallen by the wayside, while MLSs and their members seemed to sit back and watch cautiously.

This phenomenon was probably caused by a combination of two factors:

1. Limited percentage of connected members made demand low.
2. Product quality and support levels were suspect due to a very limited number of known, established vendors offering such solutions.

In other words, the biggest MLS vendors were not first out of the gate with Internet-based products. This led to a limited marketplace for the newcomers (remember, MLS contracts are generally multiyear agreements).

Today, this is all changing for the better. The established vendors with the largest market share are now offering Internet access to the older legacy systems. Some are even introducing new versions that are only available through the Internet.

■ THE RETS WORKING GROUP

One of the important events of the past few years was the establishment of the **RETS (Real Estate Transaction Standard)** working group (made up of vendors, NAR representatives, and technologists). This group set out to define a structure for the dreamed-about online Transaction Management System. This structure defines the data elements and structures for allowing data from many different locations and owned by many different participating entities to be brought together **on-the-fly** to create an effective Transaction Management System via the Internet.

A critical part of this definition has been to establish a clear set of structures under which any MLS can map its own unique data sets into a structure that can be generically combined and viewed by other MLSs with their own unique structures. Why is this such a big deal? The answer is the countless different ways property can be described—one could call it a family room, another might call it a den. Waterfront might be important to some areas, but not to an inner-city MLS. One MLS might force square footage, another might not allow it in the listing. The differences are vast and almost never-ending.

With the advent of the extensible markup language (XML), the need to have all data start out in a common structure is no longer an issue. XML is a way to map different data labels (den and family room) to a generic structure that all can understand, as the search or request is made. This requires that all parties agree on the design of the generic structure. This determination of the data model structure has been a function of the RETS-WG (RETS working group). Now, products can be and are being designed to accommodate the RETS data model. This could, of course, allow for conversion to the new Internet-based system from nearly any current MLS design. It could also, perhaps, ultimately lead to a form of national MLS—but that is a whole different topic.

What does all of this mean to the professional? It is simple. If your listings require that you get connected to the Internet, all members of an MLS will be forced to connect. Of course, the new real estate professional will have a distinct advantage due to the knowledge gained through technology training. Also, your Internet skills will become more important every day.

http://RETS.RealTown.com

Chapter Links:
http://DigitalCameras.RealTown.com
http://VirtualTours.RealTown.com
http://PersonalDigitalAssistants.RealTown.com
http://PersonalProductivitySoftware.RealTown.com
http:// LockBox.RealTown.com
http://DigitalDocumentManagement.RealTown.com
http://MLSInformation.RealTown.com
http://RETS.RealTown.com

■ REVIEW QUESTIONS

1. (T/F) Buyers want to view images of properties when searching the Internet.

   Answer: True.

   Buyers continue to indicate their preference for more property images on the Internet. As a matter of fact, your listings probably have a better chance of being the request of buyers if you use more pictures to showcase the listings.

2. Name three different brands of personal productivity software.

   Answer:

   Outlook
   Online Agent
   Goldmine
   Top Producer

3. What is meant by a virtual tour?

   Answer: A virtual tour is a series of 360°, wide angle panoramic or still photos combined with captions, and in some cases unlimited text descriptions and a streaming voice narration, that can be viewed over the Internet. These virtual tours are typically linked directly to your online listing on your Web site and other Web sites where your listing is exposed (your MLS, *Realtor.com*, Yahoo!, etc.).

Chapter Seventeen

Creating a Personal Technology Plan of Action

A dream is what you would like your life to become. A goal is what you are truly willing to do to achieve what you really want.
DENIS WAITLEY
http://Motivation.RealTown.com

Most real estate professionals purchase technology products and services in a haphazard manner, wasting precious time and monetary resources on technologies they have no business buying. The speed of invention in the technology world is mind-numbing, and every piece of hardware or software you purchase has a learning curve. **Don't buy technology until you are ready to put it to work and only as it fits into your personal technology plan of action.**

We are fortunate to live in a time that is unlike any other in recent history. The invention of the transistor, followed by the **microprocessor** and finally by the Internet, makes this a very exciting time to be alive. Let's list a few examples:

Cellular communications
Internet
E-mail
GPS (Global Positioning Systems)
Computerized automobile engines
Robotics in manufacturing and science
Personal computers
Handheld computers
Digital imaging (photography, video)

You could probably list even more examples than these in a few minutes. These and other technologies didn't exist even 50 years ago (some didn't exist 20 years ago).

Of course, we are often tempted to buy the latest and greatest whiz-bang tool for our business. Sometimes we buy it because our competitor has it. Sometimes we buy it because our client asked about it. Other times we buy it because we think it is a good thing to have. Finally, we often buy these tools for their wow factor. Unfortunately, when we get back to the office with our new tool, we somehow never find the right time to learn how to use it, set it up, or load it with our information. As a result, it gathers dust for so long we often sell or donate it in its original packaging.

What happened? We were convinced that this new tool would make us more efficient, effective, and an all-around better professional. The answer is usually simple. What happened was that the tool dictated the plan, instead of the plan dictating which tools and in what order we would invest in them. Clearly, the plan must be created first, if the tools are to be of maximum value to your business.

■ PUTTING TOGETHER A TECHNOLOGY PLAN OF ACTION

To create a personal technology plan of action requires analyzing your current business. To get the most out of technology, you want to integrate technology solutions into what you are already doing, and then employ technology in new areas. Pull out your last five transactions and list everything you did in each of the following areas (five phases of the real estate sales process):

1. Educate—The first thing you do with buyers and sellers alike is educate them about the market, the process, the disclosures, the forms, etc.
2. Locate (buyers)/Market (sellers)—What are all the things you do during this critical phase of the home buying/selling process?
3. Negotiate—You negotiate from writing the offer to presenting and countering.
4. Administrate to the closing—Many details are attended to in this phase of the process.
5. After the sale communication—How do you plan to stay in touch?

In each of the above areas, what is it exactly that you do? List everything, leaving nothing out. You will consider each technology product or service you contemplate purchasing based on where you will use it in your business.

http://RealEstateSalesCycle.RealTown.com

Now ask yourself the following question:

1. Where are you now? Complete a technology audit that includes:
   a. Type of computer and capability (processor/RAM/storage/modem/CD-RW)
   b. Type of connectivity
   c. Domain name(s)
   d. List of Internet hosts
   e. All technology tools, their manufacturers, models, and capability

http://TechAudit.RealTown.com

2. Where do you want to be with the implementation of technology and over what period of time?
3. What is your tolerance for learning as all technologies have a learning curve? How much time each day can you allocate to learning?
4. What do you want to achieve? What are your specific objectives?
5. What is your annual budget for technology?

With the above considered:

Determine your business needs and objectives
Determine your business goals
Determine the technology solutions to accomplish the goals
Determine the cost of the technology solutions
Estimate the learning curve
Determine the timeline to purchase
Create a budget for implementation
Finalize the implementation timeline
Enter dates in your calendar to give you the time to learn
Implement the plan

To create a plan, you have to uncover your business needs and objectives, first in general terms and then more specific. You will then be able to move on to establishing your business goals and looking at what technology will help you achieve those goals. Use the following outline to help you establish your needs and objectives. Note that this is just an example. You should develop your own unique **needs** and **objectives** statement.

DETERMINING YOUR OBJECTIVES

Needs and Objectives (General): More business
Needs and Objectives (Specific):
    More buyer prospects
    More seller prospects
    Better farm penetration
    Higher referral rates from client base
    Higher referral rates from associate base
    Client growth and investment marketing penetration

Needs and Objectives (General): Better business efficiency
Needs and Objectives (Specific):
    Shorter sale-to-close time frame
    Faster response to client requests
    Better client access to my team and me
    Faster access to all transactional information

Needs and Objectives (General): Better client service
Needs and Objectives (Specific):
    More client feedback
    Incidence tracking
    Better quality marketing materials
    Maximized property exposure
    Better feedback from potential buyers

Needs and Objectives (General): Better management of service vendors
Needs and Objectives (Specific):
    No missed appointments
    Faster response to inspection repair requirements
    Fewer surprises from inspections
    Better tracking of vendor quality

DEVELOPING YOUR BUSINESS GOALS STATEMENT

After completing a needs and objectives analysis, you are prepared to develop your Business Goals Statement. Goals should be written and as clear and measurable as possible. Vague goals can lead to vague results. The closer your stated measurements are to reality, the more likely you will be to attain your goals.

Question: What does my business need that technology can provide?

Needs and Objectives (General): More business
Goal: 30 percent increase in sales by January 1 (choose either an increase in the number of transactions or an increase in the dollar volume of your business)

Needs and Objectives (Specific): Better business efficiency
Goal: No increase in staff to reach the goal of more business

Needs and Objectives (General): Better client service
Goal: One referral per two clients

Needs and Objectives (General): Better management of service vendors (title companies, inspection companies, lenders, etc.)
Goal: Create and use VendorTalk Listserv for preferred vendors

■ DETERMINING YOUR SOLUTIONS

Using your needs and objectives analysis, you can list technologies that will help you attain the goals.

Possible Technology Solutions. How does each technology solution help you attain your goals as stated?

Hardware
Computer—Desktop computer or laptop computer?
CD-RW drive (with blank CDs and a label maker)
Backup device
Carrying case
Cell phone with Internet capability
Copier with legal size capability and enlarge/reduce feature
Printer—Inkjet printer or **laserjet printer**
Digital camera with wide angle lens capability, good battery life, ease of use and transfer

Docking station for laptop, if desired

Electronic lock box

Monitor

Mouse of choice

PDA, Palm, handhelds

Scanner

Surge protector, portable as well as household

Fax

Software (not in any order)

A graphics design program, or just Flash or Shockwave

Ad Writer Software including the FREE Palm Walkthru Checker

Adobe Acrobat Distiller to convert files to .pdf for CD burning and Web

Adobe PageMaker or other desktop publishing software

Backup software

Contact management software

E-mail software (Eudora Pro or Microsoft's Outlook)

ftp software to upload Web site pages/files/information

Image editing software

MS Publisher (for designing marketing materials)

Newsletters/special printing projects

Online transactions

PowerPoint

Publishing software

Quicken/QuickBooks

Real estate information management software system such as Top Producer/Agent 2000

Windows

Word

Zip Utility (Winzip, PKZip)

Services

Domain hosting

E-mail hosting

Web site hosting

Instant messenger (IM)

A technologically proficient assistant

E-Fax toll-free account

Express package/parcel delivery service (Airborne or FedEx)

Follow-me phone number that you will have forever,
for marketing purposes

Just listed/Just sold/farming postcard printing and mailing service
Online forms
Online communities
Specialized printing service (*expresscopy.com*)
Virtual tours
Web-based photo storage and the ability to send links to clients
Web site (or multiple sites)

Knowledge and Skills
Ability to send and receive digital files, photos, etc.
Advanced people skills for the younger than-30 buyer
Advanced e-mail skills
How to set up signatures and sort incoming e-mail
Web page creation/understanding
How to load property photos on Web site

ESTABLISH A TECHNOLOGY BUDGET

Buying technology tools can be a very expensive undertaking, requiring your time and money. Shopping for price can help, but be cautious not to purchase a particular brand just because it is the least expensive. Not all choices within a particular software category are the same: there are Web site development tools that are elegant and powerful just as there are similar tools that aren't worth the CD they are stored on. Digital cameras vary so much in price and power that an entire course could be written on how to best shop for a camera. This range in price and features is also true for hardware, software, and services.

> **■ TIP**
> Internet Planning Priorities Checklist
> - Own your own domain.
> - Obtain a reliable, full-featured e-mail account.
> - Create a permanent e-mail address.
> - Investigate broadband options in your area.
> - Learn and begin to use more of the functionality of your e-mail software.
> - Build your e-mail address book.
> - Web site strategy and Web marketing plan.
> - Examine Web options and allocate annual budget.
> - Make a Web site decision—make sure you can measure results.

IMPLEMENTING YOUR PLAN OF ACTION

Review your objectives, solutions, budget, and priorities. Work slowly and methodically, and stay on course to achieve your goals. Good luck.

Chapter Links:
http://RealEstateSalesCycle.RealTown.com
http://TechAudit.RealTown.com

■ REVIEW QUESTIONS

1. Creating a Technology Plan of Action requires five initial considerations; name them.

   Answer:

   Where are you now?

   Where do you want to be with the implementation of technology and over what period of time?

   What is your tolerance for learning, as all technologies have a learning curve?

   What do you want to achieve?

   What is your annual budget for technology?

2. What are the five phases of the real estate sales process?

   Answer:

   Educate
   Locate/Market
   Negotiate
   Administrate
   Communicate

3. Describe several important aspects of goals and goal setting.

   Answer: Goals should be written and as clear and measurable as possible. Vague goals can lead to vague results. The closer your stated measurements are to reality, the more likely you will be to attain your goals.

Chapter Eighteen

Competing To Win as the New Real Estate Professional

The winners in life think constantly in terms of I can, I will, and I am.

DENIS WAITLEY
http://Motivation.RealTown.com

■ THE NEW REAL ESTATE PROFESSIONAL

Salespeople and brokers alike appear overwhelmed by all the choices computers and technology offer. Emerging from the stress and confusion generated by countless choices is a new breed of real estate professional. What do these new real estate professionals look like and how do they differentiate themselves from their competition? Let's take a look at YOU as the new real estate professional.

AN INFORMATION SPECIALIST

As the new real estate professional, you recognize that the hottest commodity in the real estate business is information. Consumers can become overwhelmed and confused by the information overload generated by the Internet. You are adept at extracting information from the Internet and the local and/or regional MLS and then reassembling the information into knowledge, thus creating value for the consumer.

You will add value to the transaction in the ways you handle information for the property buyer and seller. What are the things you can do with information?

Filter
Sort
Customize
Manage
Analyze
Correlate
Process
Display
Disseminate

For example, you can e-mail a comparative market analysis along with digital photos and key public record information, such as taxes and building permits. As the new real estate professional, you are in the information business!

A WEB SURFER

Armed with a computer and Internet access, you are now an integral part of the new world of doing business within the online community. With the real estate industry in the early phases of doing business online, you are leading the charge. Although no one has all the answers on how to best use the Internet as a tool to market products and generate revenue, you continue to experiment with new approaches every day—and you are steadily finding success with consumers online.

AN E-MAIL USER

You are an e-mail powerhouse. No more telephone tag, time zone concerns, long distance charges, interrupted conversations, or piles of unanswered correspondence.

E-mail is one of the most effective marketing, advertising, risk reduction, and communication tools available in business. With a click of the mouse, and then a copy and paste of some hot news reports, you easily create a personal **electronic newsletter** filled with solid content. Another click brings up a distribution list of hundreds of clients/ prospects with e-mail addresses around the globe; another click and the e-newsletter is sent instantly to the computer of everyone on your list. No stamps to lick, no envelopes to stuff. All at the push of a button, at the speed of light.

You are sure to display your permanent e-mail address on business cards, letterhead, vehicle plates, car magnets, billboards, sign riders, property ads, and even mention it on your voice mail message. You actively solicit the e-mail address of every potential client and prospect—capturing e-mail addresses with permission becomes an important daily task. You check for e-mail messages as frequently as checking for voice mail (if not more often) and then make sure to respond promptly, recognizing that consumers are not going to wait before contacting another real estate licensee.

A WEB SITE TO BRAG ABOUT

Recognizing that content is king, you develop a Web site employing useful hypertext links (an electronic cross-reference) to other Web sites—the idea being to showcase your professionalism and expertise. You endeavor to keep the material fresh and updated, perhaps sending e-mail alerts when updates are made so consumers are encouraged to bookmark and revisit your site regularly. Listing information is the key to a stickier Web site so make sure you are familiar with your local MLS rules pertaining to Internet Data Exchange and Virtual Office Web Sites (IDX and VOW).

You view your Web site as a publishing vehicle, though never more important than word of mouth and good service. Consumers locate the Web site by using any one of the several branded domain names you've registered and which all point to your main site.

WORK FROM A MOBILE OFFICE

As a new real estate professional, your office comprises all the devices you carry with you. There is the cellular phone; the pager; the laptop with modem; the fax; the wireless Blackberry; the PDA (personal digital assistant) handheld device (containing the complete MLS inventory and access to the electronic lock box); the programmable financial calculator; the scanner; and the portable printer. Your computer can dial into the company computer and receive messages, fax MLS listings, and access other helpful data. Meetings and conferences are conducted more efficiently online through e-mail and passworded company bulletin boards on the company Intranet. There are fewer and shorter live meetings to attend because most of the background information, agendas, confirmations, updates, and follow-up are handled online.

FOCUS ON GROWTH, SELF-DEVELOPMENT, AND NEW SKILLS

You remain aware of the major cultural changes occurring in the information age. You work to develop clients and prospects who are comfortable maintaining an electronic rapport with a competent real estate professional—one who can keep the client up to date with e-mail, newsletters, property photos, and transaction documents transmitted electronically. You use traditional as well as electronic techniques to provide clients and prospects with local community information and resources.

You are able to complete the mandatory state-approved continuing education requirements through computer-based education courses when offered online in various states. You tune into private networks for online interviews and seminars by panels of national experts. As an association member, you now have a way to make leadership account-able online for some of their decisions. (Talk about grass-roots partici-pation!) Each member has a clear voice in the process.

USE A TECHNICAL REAL ESTATE ASSISTANT

You might consider hiring a virtual assistant, an individual who is highly skilled in all phases of real estate technology and the Internet. Some offices will have a professional assistant assigned to several lic-ensees. It's likely these assistants will be former real estate associates who have focused their energies on understanding and applying the new technology to enhance their employer's business practice. The assistant will also be responsible for performing backups to protect valuable information and files stored in the computer. In some cases, the virtual assistant may operate from another part of the country.

http://VirtualAssistant.RealTown.com

ENGAGE THE CONSUMER

For better or worse, the days of the real estate mortician are gone forever. You know the real estate morticians—they are the real estate licensees who throw buyers into the back seat of the car and drive them around until they are dead. No more! Today's connected consumers want to be actively engaged in the process. Moreover, they demand that the real estate salespeople working on their behalf add real value to the transaction. For the selling consumer, that means interpreting and applying the wealth of information in their best interests. For the buying consumer, that means finding and sharing property information quickly and efficiently to prevent loss of opportunity.

JOIN ONLINE COMMUNITIES AND USE LISTSERVS/MAILING LISTS

Welcome to the community of the world, a world where the new real estate professional can choose to associate and communicate with different groups of people at the push of a button, at the speed of light, on a local connection. The Internet connects people with people. It is the network of networks.

A result of connecting people is the creation of community. Online communities are reinventing the way we communicate, learn, and share information. Individuals, associations, and businesses are discovering the power, versatility, and affordability of Internet communities as a reliable resource for information on just about any topic you can imagine. Listservs, created using Internet-based software, are gaining in popularity in the real estate industry as a way to connect professionals to professionals and professionals to consumers. Listservs can help you bridge the communication gap.

http://OnlineCommunities.RealTown.com

YOU ARE A MASTER NETWORKER

You will participate online with several discussion groups networking with professionals and consumers sharing common interests—perhaps a group of commercial brokers, buyer brokers, real estate attorneys, or educators. It is like being at a national convention

365 days out of the year. It pays to network. Online networking is just another way of expanding key contacts.

PARTICIPATE IN AN ONLINE BUSINESS NETWORK

As your business moves from paper-based commerce to electronic commerce, the players in the typical real estate transaction become linked electronically. Available transaction management systems will streamline the processing and closing of the transaction. You become an expert transaction manager. On command, you can alert the appraiser, surveyor, attorney, home inspector, title company, and lender via e-mail to start work and to submit reports and documents electronically. Those players who are not up to date with the new technology will not be part of the closing process—and may be looking for a different line of work.

■ TECHNOLOGY AS A TOOL OF THE TRADE

Even though you are the new real estate professional, you still keep technology in perspective. Some days you find yourself using a No. 2 lead pencil more than your laptop. You use the computer to become more efficient in business; for example, to create standard presentations and computerized checklists and action plans to keep track of deadlines, creating a paperless trail for each transaction. The tools enable you to gather much of the needed transaction information—and less time spent tracking down information translates into more face-to-face time with qualified clients. With new mapping software, much of the statistical information about a property (surrounding schools, comparable sales, taxes, census, and environment) can be quickly assembled into an attractive graphical presentation piece.

■ WINNING WITH TECHNOLOGY

Winning with technology is more than the technology, it is a state of mind. Will you ever learn it all? It doesn't matter. The technology will continue to change faster than your capability to keep up with it. Still, you can always stay one step ahead of the competition, and that's the whole idea.

As Dr. Denis Waitley says:

"Beginning is half done!"

http://Motivation.RealTown.com

Chapter Links:
http://VirtualAssistant.RealTown.com
http://OnlineCommunities.RealTown.com
http://Motivation.RealTown.com

■ REVIEW QUESTIONS

1. What is the hottest commodity in the real estate business?

   Answer: Information

2. Name some of the things you can do with information.

   Answer:

   Filter
   Sort
   Customize
   Manage
   Analyze
   Correlate
   Process
   Display
   Disseminate

3. (T/F) Winning with technology requires more than just knowing about the technology.

   Answer: True.

   Winning with technology is as much a state of mind as it is the technology.

Check your favorite quick tips.

❏ Purchase your own domain.

❏ Purchase pointer domains.

❏ Use auto responders.

❏ Use listservs as electronic newsletters.

❏ Include a marketing message in your signature and automate your signature.

❏ Change your return address to reflect your domain name.

❏ Put your e-mail address and Web site address on your business cards and marketing materials—make sure you use your domain in both.

❏ Use unlimited e-mail addresses to track:
  1. Advertising;
  2. Spam; and
  3. Listing Tool.

❏ Purchase a digital camera—build a digital database.

❏ Build your e-mail address book:
  1. Ask for it on your voice mail.
  2. Ask for it at open houses.

❏ Create folders in your e-mail software to sort your customer-related or transaction-related e-mail—a folder for each buyer and listing.

❏ Don't rely on search engines to bring traffic to your site.

❏ Realize the Internet is a publishing vehicle.

❏ Use your current direct mail and marketing programs to collect e-mail addresses and drive traffic to your site.

❏ Join online communities; sign up for RealTalk.

❐ Have your e-mail forwarded to the POP Account of your choice.

❐ Create an online newsletter strategy.

❐ When e-mailing to a large group of addressees, make use of the "bcc" field to hide the e-mail addresses from the rest of the world.

❐ Know the number of addressees your ISP will allow you to send to in one message.

❐ Check your e-mail as often as you check your voice mail and respond promptly.

❐ Back up your work.

❐ Save your work (CTRL + S).

❐ Reboot before calling tech support.

❐ Hit Refresh when looking at Web sites previously visited.

❐ Practice safe computing:
Firewall:
    Software
    Hardware
Anti-Virus Software:
    Use automatic live update feature.

❐ On your Web site and e-mail, include:
Name of broker, and
License status.

❐ On your Web site and in e-mail, do not violate:
Fair Housing Laws;
Truth in Lending; or
RESPA.

❐ Do not advertise another broker's listing on your Web site without permission.

❐ Do not use the term REALTOR® in your domain in an unauthorized way.

❐ Know all the places your listings appear on the Internet.

❐ On your Web site, exchange value for e-mail addresses:
Free reports
Drawings (win a free digital camera)—auto-responders.

❏ Use unlimited e-mail addresses to help control spam and track advertising.

❏ Review your e-mail before you hit send.

❏ Use a vacation message when unavailable to return e-mail within 24 hours.

❏ Use e-mail to drive traffic to your Web site—"Push" to "Pull."

❏ Make money with your Web site through:

sponsors/advertisers, and
click-throughs.

❏ On your Web site:
  • Solid content;
  • Easy to navigate;
  • E-mail response form;
  • Interactive tools: reports; relo kit; e-newsletter

❏ Develop referral networks out of state through online community participation.

❏ Learn how to prospect the Internet.

❏ Include your digital marketing plan in your listing presentation.

❏ Don't give away your listing data without knowing to whom you are giving it and why you are giving it to them.

❏ Have a privacy policy on your Web site.

❏ Use Third Level Domains.

❏ Don't ask for too much personal information on your Web site unless you are offering great value in return.

❏ Never say anything in e-mail that you wouldn't want printed in the *New York Times*.

❏ Take before and after pictures of repairs; e-mail to both buyer and seller.

❏ Take a picture of included and excluded items and e-mail to sellers and buyers who made offers.

❏ Send e-mails to customers and clients with new listing info.

❏ Take pictures of clients' personal belongings for insurance purposes.

24/7/365 24 hours per day, 7 days per week, 365 days per year.
2 mbps 2,000,000 bytes per second data speed.
500 kbps 500,000 bytes per second data speed.
56K 56 thousand. Usually refers to a modem and speed of connection.
actions What an e-mail client software system must do every time a rule is activated—e.g., when messages come from *eProNAR.InternetCrusade.com*, file them in the e-PRO folder (filing them in the e-PRO folder is the *action*).
address book A facility in most e-mail client software that allows users to store address information for their contacts, recalling and using the addresses as needed.
Adobe Acrobat A series of applications from Adobe Systems that enables the user to create and view graphically oriented documents (such as catalogs, flyers, instruction manuals, presentations) and to send these to recipients who in turn can open them.
aggregators Companies that combine and offer for distribution a number of services or suite of products, usually from a variety of partners. In this context, aggregators are those companies that combine listing information from a number of sources (mostly MLSs).
always on broadband connection Cable and DSL services that allow the user to remain connected to the Internet at all times.
analog Almost everything in the world can be described or represented in one of two forms: analog or digital. The principal feature of analog representations is that they are continuous. In contrast, digital representations consist of values measured at discrete intervals.
AOL America Online.

aperture A usually adjustable opening in an optical instrument, such as a camera or telescope, that limits the amount of light passing through a lens or onto a mirror.

appliance In this context, any device that allows for connection to the Internet and the Web, including palmtops, WebTV, thin client systems, and Web-enabled cell phones.

application program An executable; that is, a program file that performs an 'execution' of code when activated, without requiring another application's intervention. Once an executable is activated, it will take action on its own. This is in opposition to data files, which require application programs to open them.

arbitration The process by which the parties to a dispute submit their differences to the judgment of an impartial person or group appointed by mutual consent or statutory provision.

ARPANET Advanced Research Projects Agency Network. The precursor to the Internet, ARPANET was a large wide-area network created by the United States Defense Advanced Research Project Agency (ARPA) in 1969.

ASCII text Also called plain text; text without formatting characters.

associated application The application that Windows uses to open a specific file type, based on default settings or the settings entered.

atoms New slang that refers to hard copy; that is, printed material.

attachment Any file attached to an e-mail message.

authentication The process of identifying an individual, usually based on a user name and password.

auto-dialers Computerized devices that automate the dialing of telephone numbers.

auto-filling When the user begins to type and the software recognizes a letter pattern, using it to fill in the rest of the word or phrase.

auto responder content Content you have made available in your auto responder.

auto responder An e-mail facility that allows you to respond automatically to incoming messages with a predetermined reply. This facility is useful when you wish to make the same information available to all who want it.

auto reply An e-mail client function that automatically sends a reply message to people who send messages to it (as in a vacation message).

auto-signature A text file appended automatically to an e-mail message.

.avi Short for Audio Video Interleave, the file format for Microsoft's Video for Windows standard.

backdoor virus Certain viruses and "worms" that enter through an undocumented way of gaining access to a program, online service, or an entire computer system. The backdoor is written by the programmer who creates the code for the program and is often known only by the programmer. A backdoor is a potential security risk.

backup device Any device that enables the user to create restorable copies of hard disk contents.

bandwidth The amount of data that can be transmitted in a given amount of time (usually stated in bits per second [bps]).

baseline The starting point; the minimum set of capabilities.

beaming Transporting digital information from one device to another by means of infrared beam technology.

bmp A bit map (often spelled "bitmap") which defines a display space and the color for each pixel or bit in the display space.

bookmark Nearly all Web browsers support a bookmarking feature that lets you save the address (URL) of a Web page (as a favorite) so that you can easily revisit the page at a later time.

broadband Maximized data transmission by use of several channels on a single wire or medium.

brochure ware Use of the World Wide Web facilities to produce graphical quality business and personal brochures; a Web site that contains mostly personal or company information.

brokerage firm A real estate company operated under the laws of a state, usually with a single responsible broker/owner or corporate license.

browser Software built on the Mosaic model that allows for translation of http, html, and other Web technologies. The software that allows a user to view and surf Web sites.

browser window The visible area within the Web browser.

bulletin board system (BBS) A collection of users gathered electronically by modem, where each person can post messages.

buyer customer A party to a real estate transaction who receives information, services, or benefits but has no contractual relationship with the REALTOR® or the REALTOR®'s firm.

cable Referring to fiberoptic cable and its use in connecting users and networks to the Internet through fiberoptic connections. Cable is a relatively fast way to connect to the Internet.

cable connectivity Connection to the Internet through the cable modem to the fiberoptic cable system.

cable modems Modems that communicate between the user and the ISP through the fiberoptic cable network.

CD-ROM (Compact Disc, Read-Only Memory) A compact disc used to store and play back computer data instead of digital audio.

central office (CO) The central telephone office a DSL user will be connecting to—usually must be less than 20,000 feet away.

certification *See* e-PRO Certification Program.

cgi (Common Gateway Interface) CGI programs are the most common way for Web servers to interact dynamically with users. Many HTML pages that contain forms, for example, use a CGI program to process the form's data once it has been submitted.

character count The total number of characters in a given field or file.

chat A form of interactive online communication in which users have real-time conversations with other people who are also online.

clean connection Access to the network that is characterized by limited or no line noise, no dropped lines, and upline/downline transmissions at or close to capacity.

client The person(s) or entity(ies) with whom a REALTOR® or a REALTOR®'s firm has an agency or legally recognized nonagency relationship.

clip A small amount of an original message's text that is clipped and pasted onto a reply to give some context to the reply.

clipboard A place in Windows where information that you have cut or copied resides. That information is stored there so you can paste it in the same document, or in another document.

community (Used in tandem with virtual communities) Offers people with similar experiences and interests the opportunity to come together, freed from the restraints of time and space, to form meaningful relationships.

community Web publishing tool A Web interface that facilitates the publishing of community-related information by visitors to the Web site.

compilation Compiled data set.

compiled data Individual data sets that are aggregated and interpolated into a single fully analyzed data set.

conditions In this context, certain parameters that an e-mail message must meet before it is acted on by a rule.

connected consumer The modern consumer who is connected to the Internet and expects to conduct business communications via e-mail and the Web.

confirmation message An auto reply that lets communicants know that you did, in fact, receive their message and will respond at some future time.

contact management system [Also referred to as Customer Relationship Managers (CRM) and Personal Information Managers (PIM)] Software that helps the user store and manage information about all of the people they come in contact with, including clients, prospects, associates, service vendors, etc.

corporate network (T1/T3) Corporate networks, usually LANs running some form of ethernet, can offer Internet access through 1.544Mbps access.

CRM (Customer Relationship Management) CRM entails all aspects of interaction a company has with its customer, whether sales-related or service-related.

CRM/PIM (Personal Information Manager) Programs that are designed to assist the user in management of contacts, appointments, activities, documents, notes, and more. *See* CRM.

cursor In this context, the cursor is the icon that identifies the location on the screen or in the document your system is focused on. Any action taken (e.g., typing over) will take place at the cursor location.

customer A party to a real estate transaction who receives information, services, or benefits but has no contractual relationship with the REALTOR® or the REALTOR®'s firm.

customization Making changes to the settings for a software system so that it behaves the way you want it to in the new default mode you define.

data sets All of the information relating to a particular record.

database Technology that allows you to store and retrieve related records and data items. In this context, database refers to the ability to store contact information, including names and e-mail addresses.

dedicated service Usually refers to an Internet access point that is only available to users on a local area network and usually provides for T1 or T3 connectivity.

deep linking Linking to any location within a Web site other than the home page.

default A setting established by the manufacturer that, if you do nothing to change it, will be part of the software.

desktop The main screen or view in the Windows environment.

desktop computer Your main computer; usually not a portable.

desktop publishing Software applications that allow the user to create publication-quality documents.

dial up Internet access that requires the use of POTS (Plain Old Telephone System) lines and relatively slow modems (usually equal to or less than 56 kbps).

dial-up networking wizard A program in Microsoft Windows that steps the user through the information gathering and setup to create an Internet connection through the user's ISP.

differentiator A characteristic that makes you unique.

digest, digest format Multiple Listserv messages compiled and sent in a single message. A digest will often have a table of contents that introduces the topics presented in each compiled message.

digest version Listserv that compiles a group of messages into a digest before sending it out to the recipients.

digital cameras Cameras that store images on digital media for later use in computerized imagery, on Web pages, for printing on personal printers, and for electronic forwarding to processing facilities.

digital data Anything (including data) that has been converted from its native form (text, as an example) into digital form (machine-readable).

digital images Images converted from traditional analog format to digital (machine-readable) format.

digitized video Video stored in machine-readable format.

distribution list *See* groups.

DNS Domain Name System; Domain Name Servers.

DNS server An Internet service that translates domain names into IP addresses. Because domain names are alphabetic, they're easier to remember. The Internet is however, really based on IP addresses.

docking station A peripheral device that allows the user to slip a notebook computer into a preconfigured slot that instantly attaches full keyboard, monitor, printer, mouse, and more to make the notebook more desktop-like.

domain A set of computers or networks sharing a common IP address.

domain host The company providing the servers on which your domain name is made available to the Internet and where your domain pointers reside.

domain name The text name corresponding to the numeric IP address of a computer on the Internet. The address or URL of a particular Web site.

domain name servers The servers where your domain is located on the Internet; a primary and a secondary server for locating your domain.

dotcom A new slang used to describe or refer to the world of the Internet. Internet-centric companies are often referred to as dotcom companies. Internet-company employees are often called dotcommers. The term is derived from the most widely held top level domain (TLD), the .com domain.

double-clicking Pressing the mouse's right or left button to create different commands.

download To transfer a file or files from one computer to another, for example, from a server to your desktop computer.

Denis Waitley Dr. Denis Waitley is one of the most respected keynote lecturers and productivity consultants in the world. He has helped millions of individuals become winners. He has studied and counseled leaders in every field, from "Fortune 500" top executives to managers of multinational corporations; from NASA astronauts to Super Bowl and Olympic champions; and from heads of government to family and youth groups; *http://DenisWaitley.com*.

drag and drop Technology that enables the user to click the mouse over an item, drag the item to a new location, and drop it into that location.

DSL (Digital Subscriber Line) DSL uses existing copper telephone transmission lines to connect users to the Internet via a central office switching node. DSL users can realize as much as 32 Mbps for downstream traffic, and from 32 Kbps to more than 1 Mbps for upstream traffic.

e-commerce (electronic commerce) A term referring to the movement of traditional financial transactions from their physical bounds to an electronic platform, such as the Internet and the Web.

E-fax Web service that enables you to send and receive faxes from e-mail.

electronic bulletin board Refers to a Web site where visitors can go to post messages, read messages, and reply to messages in a threaded, conversational fashion.

electronic envelope The "wrapper" that contains a transmitted packet of data, including the data itself and the header and routing information.

electronic newsletter The creation of and scheduled delivery through e-mail of one's professional newsletter. This can be as simple as a plain-text e-mail message or as elegant as a full Web site. Usually a newsletter should be written in a format that all recipients will be able to read (text).

electronic users' group A new phenomenon; use of the Internet for product users to be able to gather (electronically) and share insights and issues related to specific products, thus creating power as a result of their number.

e-mail Mail that is electronically transmitted by computer.

e-mail client The user-level program that allows users to access SMTP and POP functions in the virtual post offices of their ISPs or other e-mail services.

e-mail forwarding The ability to automatically forward incoming messages from your permanent e-mail address to your current ISP for retrieval.

e-mail inbox That portion of the POP server where incoming e-mail messages are accessed and downloaded.

e-mail overload When one receives so much e-mail in a time-frame that it becomes impossible to correctly read, absorb, and act upon that mail.

e-mail presence The total marketing effort, including and emphasizing branding, created using e-mail techniques including opt-in newsletters, listserv participation, e-mail signatures, and auto responders.

e-mail signatures Most e-mail systems allow the user to store one or more text files that can be appended to each outgoing message. These are commonly used for personal information, including name, phone numbers, and e-mail addresses. They can also be used for sending routine responses.

embedded link A hyperlink inserted (embedded) in a message or document.

emoticons (smileys) Emoticons are text-graphical combinations that can add certain emotional inflections to an otherwise flat e-mail message.

e-PRO certification The e-PRO technology certification program is an educational program unlike any other professional certification or designation course available, comprehensive and Interactive. It is sponsored by the National Association of REALTORS® and is specifically designed to help real estate professionals thrive in the competitive world of online real estate. In addition, the e-PRO certification course is geared to ensure continued success in online real estate after the course has been completed and certification earned, by online participation in the e-PRO community and the e-PRO referral network.

ethernet A local area network (LAN) protocol developed in 1976 by Xerox Corporation in cooperation with DEC and Intel.

e-transaction When all participants in a transaction communicate, pass documents, and share schedules and approvals totally through Internet communications—effectively speeding up the process.

executable files Program files that perform an execution of code when they are activated, without requiring another application's intervention. Once an executable is activated, it will take action on its own. This is in opposition to data files, which require application programs to open them.

extranet Closed or severely restricted access to all or part of a company's Web site, usually reserved for customers and usually requiring password authentication.

facility In this context, the physical site where servers are located, including all security features, access restrictions, backup and restore capabilities, etc.

favorite Web pages that you have saved a link to within the facilities of your Web browser for rapid retrieval.

file-size restriction Many ISPs restrict the size of any particular e-mail message. Often this can be as small as 1 MB. The message and any attachments, when broken into packets and wrapped in envelopes, will grow significantly in size. This can have a dramatic effect on the size of attachments that your recipients can receive.

firewall A specially programmed computer system used by many companies as a security measure to prevent hackers and other unauthorized users from accessing internal networks.

flame An e-mail message sent to the listserv that is especially harsh in its treatment of another member or members of the listserv community.

floppy disk Relatively old storage media; floppy disks usually contain 1.44 MB of data on a rewriteable disk.

folders The Microsoft Windows method of storage and retrieval on a hard disk.

follow-me phone number Telephone services that allow you to program an 800 number to forward calls to any number you select.

formatting bar This refers to the tool in an e-mail client that makes it possible to format message text type, fonts, character size and enhancement, message width, and more, as represented in a toolbar.

framing Bringing content from an outside Web document into your site within a subwindow of the browser. Dividing the browser display area into separate sections, each of which is really a different Web page. The net effect is to link your site to the content of another site while still keeping a part of your site on the screen.

free reports Compiled reports that you make available to Web visitors; these could include school information, MLS statistics, or demographics.

ftp (File Transfer Protocol) A method and protocol for transferring files from one point to another; typically used to upload files to a server.

full-featured e-mail account An e-mail POP account with features such as unlimited addressing, Web-based access, and auto-reply messages.

functionality The features and settings of your e-mail software that customize the system for your use.

.gif (Graphics Interchange Format) A bit-mapped graphics file format used by web designers.

gigabyte hard drive A way of measuring hard drive size in terms of how many gigabytes of data it can hold. *See* gigabyte.

gigabyte One gigabyte is equal to 1,073,741,824 bytes.

goals statement A written statement that details exactly what the success of a plan should look like, in measureable results.

GPS (Global Positioning System) A satellite navigation system used to determine terrestrial position, velocity, and time. Once exclusively used by the U.S. military, the GPS is now available to the general public worldwide. The GPS system relays satellite signals that can be processed by a GPS receiver.

group message An e-mail facility that allows you to create groups of recipients (e.g., all past clients) and send a single message to all of them at once by sending it to the group.

groups Lists of e-mail contacts and addresses you have determined belong grouped together for mass mailing purposes.

handheld calculator applications Applications on handheld devices that perform standard and scientific calculator functions.

handheld device Term currently interchangeable with palmtop device. Refers to those computing devices that are small enough to fit the palm of your hand. This is now expanded to include subnotebook computers. Same as a handheld organizer.

handheld organizer Term currently interchangeable with palmtop device. Refers to those computing devices that are small enough to fit the palm of your hand. This is now expanded to include subnotebook computers.

hard drive An important data storage medium that houses all of the electronic information and software programs on your computer.

hardened data center Ultra-secure facilities maintained by 24/7 (24 hours per day, 7 days per week) on-site personnel; each contains backup and disaster recovery systems to ensure the safety and availability of customers' applications, services, and data.

header A unit of information that precedes a piece of data; in this context, a packet. E-mail headers are used to identify source, destination, and other important information about a packet so that it can become reassembled as a message at the recipient location.

high priority Many e-mail clients allow you to assign priority to a message. A high priority says, in effect, "IMPORTANT—Read Me Now!"

homebuying process The specific steps required to move through the process of finding available properties, negotiating terms with the seller, performing inspections, arranging finances, closing, and recording the transaction within the law under generally accepted practices and principles.

home page The first page of a Web site that the visitor lands on.

hosted When a domain is registered to and located on a specific server, it is referred to as being "hosted" on that server.

hotlink A link embedded in a message or in a document that will, when clicked, transport the user to another location or will activate a program. Also known as link.

hot-port Technology that allows the user to swap different devices on a port without being required to stop the system's operation. USB is a prime example of hot-port usage.

HTML (HyperText Markup Language) The programming format that creates hyperlinks and hypermedia on Web pages.

HTTP (HyperText Transfer Protocol) The standard protocol for exchange of information on the Web.

HTTP (Hyper Text Transfer Protocol Secure) A type of server software that provides secure transactions on the Web.

hybridization Convergence of many different devices into a single configuration, such as cellular phone/PDA/camera combinations.

hyperlink A link embedded in a message or in a document that will, when clicked, transport the user to another location or activate a program.

icon A small picture or image that represents an object, a folder, or a program.

IDX Internet Data Exchange, also known as broker reciprocity.

image editing Software that enables the user to make often sophisticated changes to digital images, such as sharpening, resizing, recoloring, and much more.

IMAP Internet Message Access Protocol. An Internet e-mail protocol which allows access to your e-mail from any IMAP-compatible browser. Your mail resides on the server level while you work with it, versus POP mail which is downloaded into your mail program.

immediate Listserv that sends users each posting immediately as it comes in. *See* immediate version.

immediate version Listserv that sends you each posting immediately as it comes in.

incompatibility In this context, referring to a file that cannot be opened with existing application software on the user's computer.

independent contractor Licensed real estate professional working under the license of a brokerage in such a manner as to be able to operate independently, with little or no management being applied by the brokerage. Typically, independent contractors are not salaried employees.

information commander One whose ability to gather, manipulate, report, and analyze many forms of information through the use of modern technology is above the norm.

Information Superhighway On March 21, 1994, U.S. Vice President Al Gore described to the International Telecom Union the need to create a Global Information Infrastructure (GII), dubbed the "Information Superhighway," that would be based on five principles: first, encourage private investment; second, promote competition; third, create a flexible regulatory framework that can keep pace with rapid technological and market changes; fourth, provide open access to the network for all information providers; and fifth, insure universal service.

Instant Messenger (IM) Technology that enables users to instantly communicate with other connected users in an interactive message format.

Internet A global network connecting millions of computers and other networks.

Internet cell phones Recently developed cellular phones that are Web and e-mail enabled.

Internet Explorer The Web browser software created and distributed for free by Microsoft Corporation.

Internet service provider (ISP) The company or entity that provides a path to the Internet (Internet access) for its users. *See* ISP.

Intranet A restricted access network that operates on Web technology, usually on a closed corporate network.

IoS Short for Internet over Satellite; IoS technology allows a user to access the Internet via a satellite that orbits the Earth.

IP address A numeric address that is assigned to servers and users connected to the Internet.

ISDN (Integrated Services Digital Network) One of the fastest commercially available connections to the Internet, it is a set of communication standards that enables a single wire (or optical fiber) to carry voice, data, and video.

ISP The company or entity that provides a path to the Internet (Internet access) for its users. *See* Internet service provider.

.jpeg (jpg) Short for Joint Photographic Experts Group, and pronounced "jay-peg." Jpeg is a compression technique for color images. Although it can reduce file sizes to about 5 percent of their normal size, some detail is lost in the compression.

killer application When an application of a new technology becomes so widely accepted as to cause a massive paradigm shift, it is often called a killer application.

kiosk A boxlike unit that stands on its own and has a computer and monitor for public display. It works through a touch-screen (or built-in keyboard and pointing device) and allows customers to interact with it and make selections.

laptop A portable computer that is smaller than a desktop computer. It weighs less, is easier to carry around, and you can work on it on your lap. Also known as notebook computer.

laser printer A printer that uses a laser and dry toner to burn the printed image onto the page.

learning curve The amount of time and energy that must be invested before a technology is mastered.

library of the world The concept that the Internet offers the world community all of the collective knowledge of the world. In reality this is not the case, but there is more information available through the Internet than through any other venue.

license period The length of time a particular domain name is licensed to a domain name holder (registrant).

link A link embedded in a message or in a document that will, when clicked, transport the user to another location or will activate a program. Also known as hyperlink, hotlink.

linking A link embedded in a message or in a document that will, when clicked, transport the user to another location or will activate a program.

list owner (Also called Listserv administrator) The person or entity responsible for the management, posting, and adherence to established guidelines for a Listserv.

Listserv Mailing list software Listserv, a product of L-Soft International, Inc. The term is commonly used to describe mail-list discussions and list discussion software.

Listservs/mailing lists Those mailing lists in which the participants share a common ground (same business, etc.) and they come together through e-mail discussions using technologies like Listserv.

lurk To belong to a Listserv community but refrain from posting.

mail list Generic term meant to describe a list of names and addresses (in this case, e-mail addresses) used for bulk mailing purposes.

mailto: HTML command that tells the system to open a new e-mail message for the user.

masking Facility available to a network administrator allowing for further identification within a network. Subnet masking enables the network administrator to further divide the host part of the address into two or more subnets, effectively creating a new face for a specific page on the Internet. This is used to give a more meaningful URL to a page on the Web.

megabytes A megabyte (1 MB) represents 1,000 kilobytes, or one million bytes. (A byte is 8 bits of information.)

memory card Recently developed, very small digital storage devices that allow for large amounts of digital storage.

memory stick Microstorage devices developed and promoted by Sony Corporation for storage and transfer of digital information from one device to another.

meta-tag A special HTML tag that provides information about a Web page.

microprocessor The microprocessor handles the logic operations in a computer, such as adding, subtracting, and copying. A set of instructions in the chip design tells the microprocessor what to do, and different applications can give instructions to the microprocessor as well.

Microsoft Internet Explorer The Web browser software created and distributed for free by Microsoft Corporation.

modem Short for MOdulator, DEModulator. A hardware device you connect to your computer and to a phone line. It enables the computer to talk to other computers through the phone system. The three types of modem are external, PC card, and internal.

moderated A Listserv in which all messages pass through the Listserv administrator or manager prior to posting.

monitor In this context, a display device (like a television) that enables you to see the output of your computer.

mouse The computer device typically used to move the cursor around on the monitor. Mouse buttons are used for selection, action, and informational purposes, especially with application programs and the World Wide Web (Web).

.mov Motion image files requiring Quicktime for Windows.

Mpeg (.mpg) Short for Moving Picture Experts Group, and pronounced m-peg, a working group of ISO. The term also refers to the family of digital video compression standards and file formats developed by the group.

MSIE Microsoft Internet Explorer, the most widely used Web browser.

My Computer icon A location on the desktop to access dial-up networking, printers, available drives, and other features.

My Documents A default folder available in Windows that is usually used for storage of data files.

NAR technology certification program The e-PRO certification course.

national ISP An ISP that offers points of presence (PoP, not to be confused with Post Office Protocol) available through local phone numbers in a majority of U.S. locations.

needs statement A written statement that details exactly what you are trying to solve, accomplish, or gain.

Netscape The Web browser owned, maintained, and made available by AOL.

new real estate professional Today's real estate agent who is equipped with technology and is comfortable with its application in real estate practice.

no-brainer Something that is a "must do" or requires no thought is said to be a no-brainer.

node An intermediate processing location on a network. Nodes are usually created in order to group users on a network for resource sharing.

nodes In networks, a processing location.

noise-to-content ratio The amount of nonessential messages sent through the Listserv. Many participants are too quick to post messages like, "I agree with you" or like "Me, too." These messages are considered to be noise-level.

NRDS National REALTORS® Database System. A searchable database system with information on all members of NAR.

offline Happening or taking place without being connected to the Internet.

off-list Communicating directly (without going through the Listserv) with members of a Listserv community.

on the fly As you go; something that can be changed or created at will and as needed is said to be created on the fly.

online The state of being connected to the Internet.

online community Used in tandem with virtual communities; gives people with similar experiences and interests the opportunity to come together online, freed from the restraints of time and space, to form meaningful relationships.

online forms Fill-in-the-blanks forms on Web pages that automatically e-mail the user input to the page owner/manager.

operating system The software that communicates with the computer processor in machine-readable code; the instruction set and rules under which all application software operates.

opt-in Offering users a way to subscribe to a mailing list.

opt-out Offering the recipients of an e-mail marketing message an easy way to unsubscribe.

packets A piece of a message transmitted over a packet-switching network.

paradigm The common set of beliefs, theories, and examples that define how subscribers view a specific topic or dogma.

paradigm shift A paradigm is a set of assumptions, concepts, values, and practices that constitutes a way of viewing reality for the community that shares that set. Any sudden and large change to a paradigm is usually called a paradigm shift.

park Temporarily locating your domain name on a server until you decide where it will ultimately reside.

password protected A site that restricts entry to those who have the correct password.

PDA/handheld Term currently interchangeable with palmtop device. Refers to those computing devices small enough to fit the palm of your hand. This is now expanded to include subnotebook computers.

permanent e-mail address An e-mail address that is derived by owning and controlling your own domain name. You can use the e-mail services of the domain host to point mail to and from this domain regardless of your actual ISP. By doing this, you no longer need to change e-mail addresses.

permanent Web site address The use of and control of your own domain name for Web site URLs, including but not limited to your main site and any and all pointer domains.

permission marketing Marketing to those who have given their consent to be marketed to, usually through an opt-in message or a field on a form.

personal technology audit The process used to determine an individual's baseline technology skill set.

personal technology plan of action Step-by-step plan designed to take one's business from a starting point to a state of proficiency in targeted technologies. This plan defines the investment required, the learning curve, the resources, and the people needed for the business to become technologically competitive.

photo editing Software that enables the user to make often sophisticated changes to digital images, such as sharpening, resizing, recoloring, and much more.

PIM (Personal Information Manager) Program designed to assist the user in management of contacts, appointments, activities, documents, notes, and more.

PIN (Personal Identification Number) Your unique identifying number for security purposes, as used in banking and other applications.

ping (Packet Internet Groper) A utility that determines whether a specific IP address is accessible. Ping is used to check Internet connections by sending a packet to a server several times, testing the connection and response times.

plain text ASCII standard text; nonformatted text.

point-and-click User interface in which a user typically points to an object on the screen and then clicks a button on the mouse to take an action or to move to another location (as in hypertext).

pointer domains In this context, a pointer domain is a domain name that is used to point to the main domain. Many organizations have registered multiple variations of their domain name (including misspellings), which they then point to their base domain name through the use of pointers or redirects.

POP Account Post Office Protocol account, which enables the user to receive e-mail.

POPs Post Office Protocol servers.

pop-up window A window that appears within another window and provides information or advertising.

portals A door or entry point to a wide-ranging variety of Web sites. Used in the real estate context, a real estate portal offers a repository of industry-related Web links that provide single-click access to many real estate Web sites.

post To compose an e-mail message and send it to a Listserv for distribution to the group.

post information Cause information (data) to become part of a database or data file.

privacy statement The written stated practices of a Web site or Web company that specifies the degree of privacy and confidentiality the company or site owners will apply to the protection of the private and personal information of its users and visitors.

protocol A predetermined and common format for transmitting data from one point (computer, network, user, device) to another.

push Internet terminology used to refer to the act of putting information in front of the user, often through automated electronic communications, including e-mail newsletters, HTML-based e-mail, and Web clipping.

.qt (QuickTime) A method of storing sound, graphics, and movie files. *See* .mov.

quantummail.com An online mailing service with real estate-specific products.

real estate professionals Those who derive their primary income from a real estate business; licensed salespeople and brokers whose primary income is derived from the real estate business.

real time When something is happening on an interactive basis (action now, result now) it is often called real time.

RealTalk Digests The RealTalk Listserv as delivered in digest format.

redirecting e-mail A mail server function that enables you to automatically redirect (reflect) e-mail sent to one address to another address of your choosing.

referring agents Agents from one geographic location or who specialize in a particular practice, referring a prospective customer to real estate professionals in another location or having another specialization, often for a predetermined fee.

registrant The company or entity requesting the registration of a particular domain name.

registrar The company or entity granted the rights to register domain names.

registrars Those companies and entities granted rights to assign domain names within a TLD.

registry key Unique identifier that enables the holder to make changes to a domain registration.

registry key number Unique number assigned to a registered domain registration.

resolutions The density/quality of the display on the monitor, usually measured in pixels per inch.

RETS (Real Estate Transaction Standard) The new open standard for exchanging real estate transaction information. Consists of a transaction specification and a standard Extensible Markup Language (XML) Document Type Definition (DTD); RETS is being implemented by many real estate industry leaders in their next generation of real estate information systems.

Rich Text Format (RTF) The Rich Text Format standard is a method of encoding formatted text and graphics for easy transfer between MS-DOS, Windows, Windows 95, OS/2, and Apple Macintosh applications.

right click Pressing the mouse's right button to access commands.

risk reduction technique Any activity or technique that reduces the professional's exposure to liability for his or her actions, errors, or omissions.

robotics (robots) Computerized devices that can react to sensory-like input; they are widely used in manufacturing to perform precise and repetitive tasks.

root servers A computer or device on a network that manages network resources.

router On the Internet, a device (or, in some cases, software in a computer) that determines the next network point to which a packet should be forwarded toward its destination. A router maintains a table of the available routes and their conditions and uses this information—along with distance and cost algorithms—to determine the best route for a given packet. Typically, a packet may travel through a number of network points with routers before arriving at its destination.

routing The process of moving a packet of data from source to destination.

rules Those standards established in the e-mail client for automatic handling of incoming messages based on predetermined conditions.

scanner A device that can read text or illustrations printed on paper and translate the information into a form the computer can use.

screen capture Use of technologies designed to make a photo-like image of the computer screen's contents.

scrolling The act of moving the scroll bar in a program's active display window.

search engine A program that searches documents for specified keywords and returns a list of the documents where the keywords were found.

Second Level Domain That unique name (domain name) that identifies a particular computer or network on the Internet. It is the unique name assigned within a domain (i.e., *eProNAR.com*) and is registered with the domain registry.

server A computer or device on a network that manages network resources.

shrink-wrapped Refers to traditional manufacturing process that results in a product in a shrink-wrapped box.

signature A text file that you append to your messages; contains static information, including name, e-mail address, telephone information, etc.

site management software Software that automates the creation and maintenance of a Web site.

SLD Second level domain

SMTP (Simple Mail Transfer Protocol) The standard e-mail transmission protocol for the Internet.

SMTP server (Simple Mail Transfer Protocol server) The server software that manages all outgoing e-mail from users.

snail mail Traditional paper mail via the U.S. Postal Service.

source code The code that defines a Web page: HTML, dhtml, asp, others. Program instructions in their original form.

spam Internet junk mail; unsolicited e-mail.

speed Measured by the amount of time data can be uploaded and downloaded by a user.

sphere of influence Those people in your circle of friends, family, associates, and others with whom you are in contact.

Sputnik The first satellite to orbit the earth, launched by the USSR on October 4, 1957.

standard buttons The basic set of features, represented by toolbar buttons, that you need to have available.

stitched/stitching Joining of two or more digital images at common points to create a single contiguous image.

streaming video A method of making large-file video available via the Internet in which the video starts to play while the rest of it downloads in a continuous stream.

strip headers To remove or otherwise invalidate the header information from the source code of a Web page.

structures In this context, the design, data fields, and order of data in a given application system.

subscribe Add users to your recipient list so that they will begin receiving your mailings on an ongoing basis.

surf Navigation almost at random through a series of Web links, from one document or site to another.

surge protectors Electrical connectors and extension cords that reduce the amount of electrical surges and spikes that can harm sophisticated electronic circuitry.

switching facility Also called the central office location in a DSL system.

symmetric DSL A digital subscriber line in which the same data rates exist for both upstream and downstream traffic.

synchronization, synchronizing data Bringing the content of two devices into parity. Refers to the process of bringing all common data current between a handheld device and a desktop/laptop computer.

synergy The interaction of two or more agents or forces so that their combined effect is greater than the sum of their individual effects.

TCP/IP (Transmission Control Protocol/Internet Protocol) TCP enables two hosts to establish a connection and exchange streams of data. TCP guarantees delivery of data and also guarantees that packets will be delivered in the same order in which they were sent.

technology investment The amount of time, effort, and resources required to become proficient in those technologies that add value to one's business or services.

technology learning curve The amount of time and effort required to go from a position of no knowledge to a position of proficiency with any technology tool (hardware, software, or peripheral).

technology plan of action A stated plan for adding technology solutions to your real estate business.

text size Text is measured in font sizes as represented by the number of points a character will have in height. The more points, the larger the text.

the new real estate industry A marked change in the residential real estate industry, brought about by increased consumer access to information and supportive tools by consumers.

thin client A client that runs its applications across a network from a server. A thin client is typically used when many users access the same application from a central server.

Third Level Domains The owner of an SLD (domain name) has the ability to assign specific groupings within that domain name for categorical purposes. This can apply as in the case of e-mail addresses (JohnSmith@eProNAR.com with JohnSmith being the third level) or in Web page groupings (as in *Community.eProNAR.com*), where the community pages can be segmented to allow tighter access control and for other reasons.

thread An electronic discussion that takes the form of "Message-Reply-Reply" in a threaded conversational manner.

throughput Data transfer rates; i.e., the amount of data sent to a point in a given amount of time, usually measured in Kbytes, megabytes, or gigabytes per second.

timeout Systems often log out or shut down after a specified period of inactivity; this is called a timeout.

TLD Top Level Domain: identifies the most general part of the domain name in an Internet address. A TLD is either a generic top-level domain, such as "com" for "commercial," "edu" for "educational," and so forth, or a country code top-level domain, such as "fr" for France.

tutorials Interactive learning tools allowing the student to learn by example.

ubiquitous Occurring in many disparate locations at the same time. Seeming to be everywhere at once.

unique name Within a TLD (.com, .org, .gov, .tv, .edu, etc.) there can be only one registration of any specific domain name. As an example, there can be only one *REALTOR.com*, but there can also be one *REALTOR.org*.

universal fonts Fonts that are available to most computer users. These usually include Arial, Times, TimesNewRoman, Courier, and Serif.

Unix A popular multiuser, multitasking operating system developed at Bell Labs in the early 1970s.

upload To copy a file from your local computer to a server or host system; the reverse process of download.

URL (Uniform [or Universal] Resource Locator) The URL is the Internet equivalent of an address. Your Web site's location on the Internet is found through the use of your URL (e.g., *http://www.eProNAR.com* is the URL for this course).

user name The unique name that identifies a specific user within a certain domain. In the example JohnSmith@eProNAR.com, JohnSmith is the user name.

vacation message An auto reply that you set in your e-mail system to go out to people sending messages to you while you are out of the office. Usually, it will send a message only once to each person.

vCard An electronic business card for use in e-mail authentication, infrared beaming, and more.

view Setting up your software so that it presents only those functions you wish to see at a given time.

virtual post office This refers to those facilities offered by a host that enable the user to send and receive e-mail and to control how e-mail is handled.

virtual tour technology Use of panoramic stitched photography to allow Web surfers to experience the feeling of actually being in a location (e.g., in a house).

virtual tours Recent advance in digital photography where one digital picture is stitched to one or more other digital pictures at common points to create a continuous 360° view.

VOW Virtual Office Web site.

wave (.wav) The format for storing sound in files developed jointly by Microsoft and IBM.

Web-based photo storage Web services that offer space and tools for you to upload your digital photos, making them available for your friends, family, associates, and clients to see.

Web editing Creation of pages, hyperlinks, and tools for a Web site.

Web hosting Making facilities available for location of Web pages and Web services.

Web interface An interface to a program or programs that offers the user point-and-click actions, usually through hypertext.

Web mail Web services that allow the user to manage e-mail from a Web page. This can include sending, receiving, storing, and forwarding.

Web-on-the-fly Tools that enable nontechnical users to create sophisticated Web sites by selecting from menus of content and then adding their unique information.

Web presence The total marketing effort, including and emphasizing branding, invested using the World Wide Web, including Web sites, reciprocal linking, and more.

Web response forms Fill-in-the-blanks forms on Web pages that automatically e-mail the user input to the page owner/manager.

Web site A place on the World Wide Web that's comprised of files containing text or graphics that appear as digital information on a computer screen.

Web site requests Calls to your domain from user action on Web sites. This can include incoming links as well as incoming e-mail and more.

Whois A unique database search facility that enables one to look up a domain registration record to determine ownership.

Wi-Fi A high-speed wireless networking standard, formerly known as 802.11b.

Windows for Pocket PC Microsoft's current operating system for handheld devices that uses and emulates some of the features of Windows, allowing the user to have familiar MS Office tools in a handheld configuration.

Windows Operating System The operating system developed and supported by Microsoft Corporation The most widely used operating system for personal computers.

Windows Popular operating systems for personal computing developed and maintained by Microsoft Corporation

wireless communications Transmissions that do not require physical wireline connections.

wireless e-mail Recent developments in the pager and PDA realms allow for wireless access to e-mail through devices such as the Blackberry e-mail device, the Novatel wireless modem, cellular telephones, and more.

Word Microsoft Corporation's premier word processing software.

World Wide Web (WWW) A navigational and multimedia-based presentation protocol that enables users to jump from one point on a document to another point on a document or another document (on the same server or on a different server attached to the Internet) through the use of hypertext transfer protocol (http). Users click on hyperlinks to activate the navigation, thus creating a random navigation path at runtime.

worm Short for: write once, read many. Known primarily as a virus; it is a computer program that can replicate itself.

WOW factor How much excitement an item generates based on its technology, looks, and/or price.

WWW World Wide Web.

WYSIWYG An acronym, representing What You See Is What You Get, for a technology that allows you to view or print a document exactly as it looks.

zip files Files that have been compressed by removing nonessential bits, such as zeros and blanks. Further compression is attained through a sampling algorithm that strips bits on a predetermined frequency.

Index ■

A

2 mbps, 40
24/7/365 operations, 34
56K, 39
500 kbps, 40
ACT, 191, 192
Actions, 70–71
Ad tracking, 83
Address book, 72, 91, 107, 190, 215
Administration, 200
Administrative area, 130
Administrative Contact, 24–25
Adobe
    Acrobat, 204
    PageMaker, 204
    PDF file, 161
    Reader, 196
Advanced Research Projects
  Agency (ARPA), 8–9
Advertising, 147, 154–55
After-sale communication, 200
Agent 2000, 204
AgentOffice, 191, 192, 193
Aggregator, 96, 112, 128
Amazon, 7
America Online (AOL), 44–46, 51,
  67, 129, 167
    connectivity, 46
    e-mail limitations, 47
    MLS and, 46
Analog camera, 183
Anthony Schools, 176
Anti-cybersquatting Consumer
  Protection Act, 15
Anti-scraping, 85
Antivirus software, 106, 110
AOL. *See* America Online

Apple Newton, 190
Application program, 75
Application service provider (ASP),
  114
ARELLO, 181
ARPA. *See* Advanced Research
  Projects Agency
ARPANET, 49
Arthur Young, 144
ASCII text, 56
Associated application, 75
Association communities, 170
AT&T, 42
Atoms, 148
Attachment, 40, 55, 72, 106
    file, 74–75
    opening, 107
Auto-dialer, 193
Auto-filling, 72
Auto responder, 83, 96, 137, 149,
  215
Automated signature, 64–65, 95
Autoreply, 87–88, 95
.avi, 75

B

Backdoor viruses, 107
Bandwidth, 33, 42, 74
Bcc. *See* Blind carbon copy
Berkeley Internet Name Domain
  (BIND), 11
Berners-Lee, Tim, 9, 111
BIND. *See* Berkeley Internet
  Domain
Blind carbon copy (Bcc), 73–74
.bmp, 75
Bookmark, 133, 134